VERGIL
AENEID IV

VERGIL: THE STANDING FIGURES ARE THE
MUSES OF HISTORY (LEFT) AND TRAGEDY.
(From a Roman mosaic found at Sousse, Tunisia, a town
near the site of the ancient Hadrumetum.)

VERGIL
AENEID IV

Edited with Introduction,
Notes and Vocabulary by

H.E. Gould and J.L. Whiteley

Bristol Classical Press

Cover illustration: speluncam Dido dux et Troianus eandem deveniunt (165) – Dido and Aeneas in the cave; panel from a mosaic of the fourth century AD found at Low Ham Villa, Somerset; Castle Museum, Taunton

First published by Macmillan & Co. Ltd in 1943
New edition published in 1981 by arrangement with
Macmillan & Co. Ltd by
Bristol Classical Press
an imprint of
Gerald Duckworth & Co. Ltd
The Old Piano Factory
48 Hoxton Square, London N1 6PB

Reprinted 1989, 1992, 1993, 1995, 1997

A catalogue record for this book is available
from the British Library

ISBN 0-906515-93-9

Available in USA and Canada from:
Focus Information Group
PO Box 369
Newburyport
MA 01950

Printed in Great Britain by
Booksprint, Bristol

CONTENTS

LIST OF ILLUSTRATIONS

FOREWORD

THIS edition of Vergil's Aeneid IV has been prepared
on the same principles as previous volumes in the
Modern School Classics. That is to say, the editors,
believing that the annotated classical texts of the past
generation give too little practical help in translation,
and yet at the same time have their commentaries
overloaded with unnecessary information on points
only remotely connected with the text, have sought
to write notes that will make it possible for the school
boy or girl of today, who is quite likely to begin the
preparation of the School Certificate set books without
having previously read any continuous Latin texts at
all, to produce, in reasonable time, and without the
discouragement of being baffled by difficulties, a
correct translation of passages set by their teachers
for preparation.

In these times such pupils will need a great deal of
help which in the spacious days of classical teaching
fifty years ago they were considered not to require,
and they will need moreover that such help should at
first be given repeatedly, until each difficulty of
construction becomes familiar.

The editors, bearing in mind, as they have tried to
do throughout, the difficulties experienced by present

day pupils in the study of a subject which once received a much more generous share of the time table, hope that they have done something, in the present edition, to smooth their path.

H. E. G.
J. L. W.

WELLINGBOROUGH, 1943.

Note to the Bristol Classical Press edition

In this edition it has been necessary to remove some of the original illustrations and, consequently to change the original pagination. New illustrations have been drawn by Patrick Harrison for the cover and pp. 25, 34 and 53 based on the mosaic from the Low Ham Villa in Somerset.

BRISTOL 1981   J.H.B.

INTRODUCTION

Publius Vergilius Maro

Vergil was born on October 15th, 70 B.C. at Andes, near Mantua in Cisalpine Gaul—the Lombardy plain. Andes is usually identified with the present Pietole, three miles from Mantua ; this identification, however, has been rejected by some modern scholars, who favour a site close to the existing towns of Carpendolo and Calvisano.

The poet's family seems to have been of some local importance, and his father, who owned and worked a farm, was able to give his son the ancient equivalent of a university education. Vergil studied at Cremona and Milan, and later went to Rome to complete his course in rhetoric and philosophy.

No doubt his father wished Vergil to make his way, as Cicero had done, by his eloquence, first in the law courts as a pleader, or barrister, and then in politics by standing as a candidate for the various magistracies which led ultimately to the consulship and a seat in the senate. Vergil's temperament, however, for he was shy, nervous and awkward in society, was quite unsuited to such a career, and after a single appearance before a jury, he decided to devote his life to philosophy and poetry.

Vergil returned to his native district, where he began

to write his first important work, the Eclogues, or
Bucolics, ten poems, in semi-dramatic form, in which
the persons are imaginary shepherds and their loves.
This fashion of poetry, called ' pastoral ', was developed
by the Sicilian Greek Theocritus.   The Eclogues made
Vergil's reputation as a poet and gained the attention
of Maecenas, who at that time was the most trusted
adviser in home affairs of Octavian, heir and successor
of Julius Caesar, and destined shortly to become master
of the Greco-Roman world as the first Roman Emperor,
Augustus.

During this period of his life, in 41 B.C., Vergil was
one of the many landed proprietors who saw their
farms ruthlessly confiscated and allotted to demobilized
soldiers—a common event during those troubled years
of civil war which preceded the collapse of the Roman
Republic.   Fortunately for the poet, however, the
fame of the Eclogues and his friendship with Maecenas
made Vergil's position secure under the new régime,
and enabled him to devote the rest of his life to poetical
composition, free from all economic anxiety, at Naples
and Nola in Campania.

Thus, in or about 37 B.C., Vergil began his second
great work, the Georgics, a long poem, in four books,
which describes the Roman methods of farming, the
production of crops, of the vine and the olive, the
breeding of stock and the keeping of bees.   As we
know from Vergil himself that he was asked to write
on this subject by Maecenas, we may safely assume

that his poem was designed as propaganda for Augustus' 'new order' in Italy, and to reinforce that emperor's attempts to revive Roman religion, Roman agriculture, and the simple but hardy virtues which had made Rome great.

The two thousand odd lines of the poem were written very slowly, the years 37–30 B.C. being devoted to their composition, and reveal the highest standard of pure craftsmanship yet reached in Latin poetry. Moreover, though his subject in this poem might seem unlikely to produce great poetry, Vergil found the theme so congenial to his nature that he overcame the many difficulties, and not only produced a valuable text book for farmers, but also wrote some of the noblest poetry in the Latin language.

Soon after the completion of the Georgics, Vergil, now 40 years of age, embarked, again no doubt at the instigation of his political patrons, upon his greatest and most ambitious work, the writing of an epic, i.e. a heroic narrative poem, the Aeneid, which should rival Homer's Iliad and Odyssey, and honour the imperial achievements of the Roman race, glorify the Roman character and focus Roman national sentiment on Augustus as the man sent by destiny to bring peace, stability and prosperity to the Greco-Roman world, racked for so many years by civil war, fear and uncertainty.

The Aeneid occupied Vergil's whole attention for the remaining years of his life. In 19 B.C., after a journey to the East, he fell ill on his return to Italy at Brundisium. His health had never been robust, and realizing that his end was near he gave instructions that the great epic, for which he had planned a three years' revision, and of whose imperfections, as an intensely self-critical artist, he was very conscious, should be destroyed. This instruction, fortunately for literature, was disregarded by the poet's literary executors.

The Aeneid is an epic poem in twelve books, and tells how a Trojan prince, Aeneas, a survivor from the sack of Troy by the Greeks, is directed by the gods to seek a new home in Italy. In that land, after many vicissitudes, he settles with his Trojan companions, and it is from these colonists that the Romans liked to believe that they were sprung. Into this legend Vergil weaves a glorification of the family of Augustus, connecting the Julian clan, to which it belonged, with Iulus, the son of Aeneas.

Criticism of the poem has always recognized its superlative artistry, despite Vergil's own dissatisfaction with its lack of final polish, and is unanimous in detecting in Vergil's mind and writings a profound sensitivity and sympathy with human troubles, hardly

paralleled in Latin literature. In so far as judgment
has been adverse, it has fastened on the character of
the hero, Aeneas himself, in whom the virtue of *pietas*,
' dutifulness ', whether towards father, country or
gods, is allowed prominence at the expense of warmer
and more human feelings.

The story of the epic, book by book, is as follows.

BOOK I. Aeneas and his companions are driven by
a storm aroused by Juno, implacable enemy of the
Trojan race, towards the North African coast, where,
thanks to the intervention of Neptune, most of the
ships find shelter, their crews landing safely and making
their way to Carthage. In this city, which has just
been founded by Dido, a young widowed princess from
Tyre, they are hospitably received by the queen, who,
at a banquet, invites Aeneas to relate the story of his
wanderings.

BOOK II. The Trojan hero begins his narrative with
the story of the final siege, capture and sack of Troy.
We hear of the feigned deserter Sinon, of the trick of
the Wooden Horse, the cruel death of Laocoon and his
sons, who sought to warn the Trojans of their approach-
ing doom, the entry of the Greeks, their murder of
King Priam, and the escape of Aeneas from the burning
city with his aged father Anchises, his young son
Iulus, known also as Ascanius, and the household gods.
In the confusion his wife Creusa is lost, but later Aeneas
meets her ghost and is told that he is destined to found
a new kingdom in Italy.

Book III.   The narrative continues with the escape
of Aeneas and his Trojan comrades from the mainland,
and their voyage to various places in search of the
' promised land '—to Thrace, Delos, Crete, and finally
to the West, by way of the Strophades Islands, and
the coast of Epirus (Albania), where Aeneas is advised
by Helenus to sail round Sicily, to make for the west
coast of Italy, and there to consult a prophetess, the
Sibyl, at Cumae, and to appease Juno.   Aeneas does
as Helenus suggests, and thus, after seven years'
wandering over the Eastern Mediterranean, he arrives
at the western end of Sicily, where he spends the winter.
Aeneas concludes his narrative to the queen, his hostess,
by recording the death in Sicily of his father, Anchises.

Book IV.   Meanwhile Dido, who has been greatly
attracted to Aeneas from the first owing to the influence
of Venus, his mother, now falls more and more deeply
in love with him.   Shortly after his arrival at Carthage,
by the power of Juno and Venus, who from quite
different motives favour such a development, Dido
and Aeneas become lovers.   Jupiter, however, now
intervenes, and warns Aeneas, through Mercury, that
he must leave Africa at once and fulfil his destined task
of founding a new realm in Italy.   Realizing the
strength of Dido's passion for him, he tries to depart
secretly, but his intentions become known to her.
Yet he remains unmoved by her entreaties, which turn
in the end to words of scorn and hatred.   As he sails
away, Dido destroys herself.

Book V. Aeneas returns to western Sicily and there celebrates the anniversary of his father's death with funeral games.[1] During the latter Juno, pursuing her relentless hostility to their race, persuades the Trojan women, weary as they are of their wanderings, to set fire to the ships, but a sudden rain-storm subdues the flames and only four are destroyed. The Trojans sail away from Sicily. On the voyage Palinurus, the helmsman, is overcome by sleep, and falling overboard, is drowned.

Book VI. In this, to many readers the finest book of the poem, Aeneas, having at last set foot on the coast of Western Italy, visits the Sibyl of Cumae and

From coins struck by the Carthaginians during their occupation of Sicily. One shows a horse's head and a palm-tree, the other the head of a woman, possibly Dido. (British Museum.)

receives from her directions for the visit he longs to pay to the underworld. Armed with the ' golden bough ', which alone can procure him access to the nether regions of Hades, he traverses the various

[1] The elaborate account of these games, which occupies most of Book V, is no doubt due to the influence of Homer, who in the Iliad describes at great length the funeral games of the hero Patroclus.

quarters of that kingdom and meets the spirit of his
father, who parades for Aeneas the souls of all great
Romans that are awaiting incarnation.[1]   In this way
Vergil is able to give his readers a kind of national
cavalcade of all the great figures in Roman history from
the earliest times down to his own day.   Thus the
pageant closes with the greatest figure of them all,
the emperor Augustus.

The sixth book contains the famous lines (851–3),
which epitomize the Roman's pride in the city's
greatness as an imperial power :

> Tu regere imperio populos, Romane, memento ;
> Hae tibi erunt artes ; pacisque imponere morem,
> Parcere subiectis, et debellare superbos.

> ' Thou, O Roman, remember to rule the nations 'neath thy
>   sway.
> These shall be thine arts, to impose the laws of peace,
> To spare the conquered and to chasten the proud in war.'

BOOK VII.   Aeneas at last enters his promised land
by the mouth of the river Tiber, the natural frontier
between the districts of Latium, lying south of the
river, and Etruria to the north.   He is welcomed by
Latinus, king of Latium, who sees in Aeneas the
bridegroom for his daughter Lavinia, for whom he
has been advised by an oracle to find a foreign husband.

Turnus, however, chieftain of the neighbouring
Rutuli, and goodliest of Lavinia's suitors, is enraged

---

[1] Note again Vergil's indebtedness to Homer. Odysseus,
too, in Book XI of the Odyssey, is made to visit the underworld.

at the proposal of Latinus, and supported by Amata, the latter's queen, arouses the Latins against the Trojans. The book closes with a magnificent catalogue of the Italian forces—another epic convention, originating in Homer's catalogue of the Greek ships in the Iliad, Book II.

BOOK VIII. The river god Tiberinus sends Aeneas to seek aid from a Greek, Evander, who has settled on the Palatine Hill in what is destined to be the future Rome. Evander promises help and conducts Aeneas through the city, explaining the origin of various Roman sites and names. Venus persuades Vulcan, her husband, to make Aeneas a suit of armour, and a shield [1] on which are depicted in relief various events in the future history of Rome, down to the battle of Actium, 31 B.C., by which Vergil's patron Augustus gained undisputed sovereignty over the ancient world.

BOOK IX. While Aeneas is absent, Turnus makes an attempt, barely frustrated, to storm the Trojan camp by the Tiber, and is successful in setting fire to their ships. Nisus and Euryalus, two Trojans, endeavour to slip through the enemy lines in order to inform Aeneas of the critical situation. They slay some of the foe, but are eventually discovered and killed. The next day, when Turnus renews his assault, he succeeds in entering the camp, but is cut off, and only effects his escape by plunging into the Tiber.

[1] Homer, too, in the Iliad, Book XVIII, describes at length a shield, that of the Greek hero, Achilles.

Book X.   A council of the gods is held in Olympus and Jupiter decides to leave the issue of the war to fate. Aeneas now wins the support of an Etruscan army which has revolted against the cruelties of the king Mezentius, and joined by reinforcements from Evander under the leadership of the latter's son, Pallas, he returns to aid the hard-pressed Trojans.   In the furious fighting, Mezentius and his son Lausus are slain, but Turnus kills Pallas.

Book XI.   A truce is arranged for the burial of the dead.   On the arrival of an embassy from the Latins, Aeneas offers to settle the issue by a single combat between himself and Turnus.   The Latins hold a council of war and determine to continue the struggle, but they are defeated a second time by the Trojans and their allies in spite of many deeds of valour, especially on the part of Camilla, a warrior maiden who is killed in the fighting.

Book XII.   Another truce is arranged, and Turnus is ready to accept Aeneas' challenge despite the opposition of the queen Amata and his sister, Juturna.   The latter provokes the Latins to violate the truce.   In the ensuing struggle Aeneas is wounded, but is miraculously healed by his mother, the goddess Venus.   He returns to the fray, routs the Latins and Rutulians and eventually meets Turnus in single combat.   The Rutulian chieftain is wounded and rendered helpless.   Aeneas is minded to spare him until he notices that he is wearing the belt of the dead Pallas, whereupon he slays him.

THE METRE OF THE POEM

Most English verse consists of lines in which stressed syllables alternate with unstressed, as for example in the lines :

'The plo͓ughman h͓omeward pl͓ods his we͓ary wa͓y,

And le͓aves the wo͓rld to d͓arkness a͓nd to m͓e.'

Such verse is called *accentual.*

The principle of Greek and Latin verse is different. It is based on the rhythmical arrangement of long and short syllables, the long syllables taking twice as long to pronounce as the short. This system may be compared with music, long syllables corresponding to *crotchets* and short to *quavers*, one *crotchet* being equal to two *quavers*. This type of verse is called *quantitative.*

Just as, to appreciate the rhythm of English verse, you are taught to *scan*, i.e. to divide the lines into *feet* and mark the stress in each foot, so you must learn to scan Latin verse by a similar division into feet and by marking the syllables long (–) or short (˘). Not only is it necessary to do this in order to understand the construction of the verse and the musical qualities of the poetry, but the ability to do so is a great help in translation, by making it possible to distinguish words alike in spelling but different in *quantity*, for example, *pŏpŭlŭs*, 'people', from *pōpŭlŭs*, 'poplar tree'.

The verses of the Aeneid are called heroic hexameters. In this verse two kinds of feet, or bars, are

found. One is the *dactyl*, a long syllable followed by two short syllables, the other, the *spondee*, two long syllables. Each line, or hexameter, contains six feet, the first four of which may be either dactyls or spondees, the fifth being almost always a dactyl, and the sixth a spondee. In place of this sixth-foot spondee a trochee (- ⌣) is allowable.

Thus the scheme of the hexameter is as follows :

1	2	3	4	5	6
– ⌣ ⌣	– ⌣ ⌣	– ⌣ ⌣	– ⌣ ⌣	– ⌣ ⌣	– –
or – –	– –	– –	– –		– ⌣

In the scansion of these lines, no account is taken of syllables at the close of words *ending* in a vowel or an *m*, if they are followed immediately by a word *commencing* with a vowel or an *h*. Such a final syllable is said to be *elided*, ' struck out ', though it was more probably slurred in pronunciation. Thus in l. 7 of the present book, which begins *umentemque Aurora*, the final *e* of *umentemque* is ignored in scanning.

*   *   *

A long syllable is one that contains a vowel long *by nature*, or a diphthong ; or a vowel, naturally short, that is long *by position*, i.e. is followed by two consonants.

A short syllable is one that contains a vowel short *by nature* and ends either with no consonant, or with only one.

The two consonants which have been mentioned

as having the effect of lengthening a syllable need not both occur in the one word. Thus, in l. 1, the final syllable of *iamdudum* is long, though the *u* is naturally short, because that *u* is followed by *m* and the *s* of *saucia.*

PROSODY

The following information about the *quantity* of Latin syllables will be found useful.

A. Relating to all syllables.

All diphthongs are long, except before another vowel.

B. Relating to final syllables.

   1. Final *a* is usually short.
   Except
      (a) in the abl. sg. of 1st decl. nouns, e.g. *mensā* ;
      (b) in the 2nd sg. imperative active of 1st conjugation verbs, e.g. *amā* ;
      (c) in indeclinable words like *intereā, frustrā.*
   2. Final *e* is usually short.
   Except
      (a) in the abl. sg. of 5th decl. nouns, e.g. *aciē* ;
      (b) in the 2nd sg. imperative active of 2nd conjugation verbs, e.g. *monē* ;
      (c) in adverbs formed from adjectives in -*us*, -*a*, -*um*, e.g. *pulchrē.* (Note, however, *benĕ, malĕ.*)
   3. Final *i* is usually long.

Except in *mihi, tibi, sibi, ubi, ibi*, in which it may be long or short, and in *quasi, nisi.*

4. Final *o* is usually long.
Except in *modo, duo, ego.*

C. Final syllables of words of more than one syllable,
ending in any single consonant other than *s*, are short.
Except

(*a*) *dispār* ;

(*b*) in the perfects *iīt* and *petiīt.*

D. 1. Final *as, os, es,* are long.
Except

(*a*) *compŏs, penĕs* ;

(*b*) in nominatives singular in *es* of 3rd declension
nouns (consonant stems) having genitive
singular in *-ĕtis, -ĭtis, -idis* : e.g. *segĕs, milĕs,
obsĕs.* (But note *pariēs, abiēs, Cerēs.*)

(*c*) in compounds of *es* (from *sum*), e.g. *abĕs,
prodĕs.*

2. Final *us* and *is* are short.
Except *ūs.*

(*a*) in gen. sg., nom., voc. and acc. pl. of 4th decl.
nouns, e.g. *gradūs* ;

(*b*) in the nom. sg. of consonant stem 3rd decl.
nouns having gen. sg. with a long penultimate
syllable, e.g. *tellūs* (*-ūris*), *palūs* (*-ūdis*),
virtūs (*-ūtis*).

And except *īs*

(*c*) in dat. and abl. pl., e.g. *mensīs, dominīs, vinīs* ;

(*d*) in nom. and acc. pl. of 3rd decl.-*i* stems,
e.g. *omnīs, navīs* ;

(*e*) in the 2nd pers. sg. of 4th conjugation verbs,
e.g. *audīs* ; and in *sīs*, and compounds of *sīs*,
as *possīs* ; and in *velīs, nolīs, malīs*, and *īs*
(from *eo*).

E. Quantity of syllables determined by position in
the same word.

1. A syllable ending with a vowel or diphthong,
immediately followed by a syllable beginning with a
vowel, or with *h* and a vowel, is short : e.g. *vĭa, prăe-
ustus, trăhit.*

Except

(*a*) in the case of genitives in *-ius*, e.g. *alĭus,
solĭus, utrĭus*. (But not *illĭus*.)

(*b*) *e* preceding *i* in 5th decl. nouns, e.g. *dĭĕi*, and
in *ĕi* (from *is*).

(*c*) the syllable *fī* in *fio*. (But note *fĭeri, fĭerem*,
the *i* being short before *er*.)

2. A syllable containing a vowel immediately
followed by two consonants, or by *x* or *z*, which are
really double consonants (*cs* and *ds*) is long ; e.g.
regent, auspex.

Except

(*a*) if the two consonants are a combination of one
of the following, *b, c, d, f, g, p, t*, with (following) *l* or *r*.

If a short vowel precedes such a combination the
syllable is not necessarily long.

Finally, it must be remembered that these rules
apply to Latin words only, and not to several Greek
proper names which will be encountered in this book.

▪   ✳   ●

Let us now see if, with the information given above, we can scan one of the hexameters of this poem.

Looking at line 19, for example,

huic uni forsan potui succumbere culpae

(i) see first whether any syllable requires to be elided, i.e. not taken into account. (In this line there is none, though elision is frequent in Vergil and must always be looked for *first*.)

(ii) Mark long (-) all syllables whose long quantity can be determined by the rules given above.

for, san, suc, cum, cul

are all long syllables (by Rule E 2).

huic, pae are long syllables because they contain diphthongs (Rule A).

The *i* in *uni* and the *i* in *potui* are long (Rule B 3). This now gives us

hūic unī forsān potuī sūccūmbere cūlpāe

(iii) Mark short all syllables whose short quantity can be determined by rule.

The *u* of *potui* and the final *re* of *succumbere* are short by Rules E 1 and B 2, giving us

hūic unī forsān potŭī sūccūmberĕ cūlpāe.

Now work backwards from the end of the line, because the pattern of the last two feet (- ⌣ ⌣ | - - or - ⌣) is constant.[1] This gives us, for these feet,

---

[1] Very occasionally a spondee is found in the 5th foot.

$$\overset{5}{|\ cumb\breve{e}r\breve{e}}\ \ \overset{6}{|\ c\bar{u}lp\bar{a}e.}$$

Working backwards again the fourth foot is obviously a spondee:

$$\overset{4}{|\ \bar{\imath}\ s\bar{u}c\ |}$$

and the third, a dactyl:

$$\overset{3}{|\ s\bar{a}n\ p\breve{o}t\breve{u}\ |}$$

it being obvious that the *o* of *potui*, preceded as we know it to be by a long syllable, and followed by a short syllable, must itself be short.

This leaves us with four syllables to be got into the two remaining feet, which must thus both be spondees:

$$\overset{\text{I}}{|\ hu\bar{\imath}c\ \bar{u}n}\ \ \overset{2}{|\ \bar{\imath}\ for\ |}$$

And the whole line, divided into feet and with the quantities marked, is

$$\overset{\text{I}}{hu\bar{\imath}c\ \bar{u}n}\ |\ \overset{2}{\bar{\imath}\ for}\ |\ \overset{3}{s\bar{a}n\ p\breve{o}t\breve{u}}\ |\ \overset{4}{\bar{\imath}\ s\bar{u}c}\ |\ \overset{5}{cumb\breve{e}r\breve{e}}\ |\ \overset{6}{c\bar{u}lp\bar{a}e.}$$

One thing remains to be done before the scansion is complete. It is a rule that usually in the 3rd foot, more rarely in the 4th, one word must end and another begin. This is called the *caesura* or ' cutting '. If this break occurs after the first syllable of the foot, the caesura is said to be *strong* ; if after the second, **weak.** In this line we obviously have a strong caesura in the 3rd foot. The caesura is regularly marked in scansion by a pair of vertical lines.

Thus the scansion of the line, as completed, is

   1   2   3   4   5   **6**

$h\bar{u}\bar{\imath}c\ \bar{u}n$ | $\bar{\imath}\ for$ | $s\bar{a}n$ || $p\breve{o}t\breve{u}$ | $\bar{\imath}\ s\breve{u}c$ | $c\bar{u}mb\breve{e}r\breve{e}$ | $c\bar{u}lp\bar{a}e.$

You will find that, with careful attention to the pronunciation of Latin words, you will gradually learn to scan by ear, without the necessity of applying for help to the rules of prosody. You should try to develop this power as early as possible.

Note that the scheme of the hexameter makes it elastic, and gives it a variable length, as long as 17 or as short as 13 syllables. This makes possible such onomatopoeic lines as

$qu\bar{a}dr\breve{u}p\breve{e}$- | $d\bar{a}nt\breve{e}\ p\breve{u}$- | $tr\bar{e}m\ s\breve{o}n\breve{\imath}$- | $\bar{\imath}u\ qu\bar{a}t\breve{\imath}t$ | $\bar{u}ng\breve{u}l\breve{a}$ |

                                              $c\bar{a}mp\breve{u}m.$

(where the poet, describing the galloping of horses, imitates the sound of them),
and as

$\bar{\imath}ll(i)\ \bar{\imath}n$- | $t\bar{e}r\ s\bar{e}$- | $s\bar{e}\ m\bar{a}g$- | $n\bar{a}\ v\bar{\imath}\ br\bar{a}cch\breve{\imath}\breve{a}$ | $t\bar{o}ll\bar{u}nt$

(where again sound is matched to sense, for the line describes the alternate blows upon an anvil delivered by two smiths).

VERGIL

AENEID IV

*Dido, Queen of Carthage, confides to her sister Anna her passion
for Aeneas, her Trojan guest, but declares her intention to
remain faithful to her dead husband Sychaeus.*

At regina gravi iamdudum saucia cura
vulnus alit venis, et caeco carpitur igni.
multa viri virtus animo, multusque recursat
gentis honos ; haerent infixi pectore vultus
verbaque, nec placidam membris dat cura quietem.   5
postera Phoebea lustrabat lampade terras,
umentemque Aurora polo dimoverat umbram,
cum sic unanimam adloquitur male sana sororem :
' Anna soror, quae me suspensam insomnia terrent?
quis novus hic nostris successit sedibus hospes?   10
quem sese ore ferens! quam forti pectore et armis!
credo equidem, nec vana fides, genus esse deorum :
degeneres animos timor arguit.   heu, quibus ille
iactatus fatis! quae bella exhausta canebat !
si mihi non animo fixum immotumque sederet   15
ne cui me vinclo vellem sociare iugali,
postquam primus amor deceptam morte fefellit ;
si non pertaesum thalami taedaeque fuisset,
huic uni forsan potui succumbere culpae.
Anna, fatebor enim, miseri post fata Sychaei   20
coniugis et sparsos fraterna caede penates,
solus hic inflexit sensus, animumque labantem

impulit : agnosco veteris vestigia flammae.
sed mihi vel tellus optem prius ima dehiscat,
vel pater omnipotens adigat me fulmine ad umbras, 25
pallentes umbras Erebi noctemque profundam,
ante, Pudor, quam te violo, aut tua iura resolvo.
ille meos, primus qui me sibi iunxit, amores
abstulit ; ille habeat secum servetque sepulchro.'
sic effata sinum lacrimis implevit obortis.					30

*Anna persuades her sister that a marriage with Aeneas cannot
	affront the dead, is desirable on political grounds, and is
	even the will of the gods.*

Anna refert : ' o luce magis dilecta sorori,
solane perpetua maerens carpere iuventa,
nec dulces natos, Veneris nec praemia noris?
id cinerem aut manes credis curare sepultos?
esto, aegram nulli quondam flexere mariti				35
non Libyae, non ante Tyro ; despectus Iarbas,
ductoresque alii, quos Africa terra triumphis
dives alit : placitone etiam pugnabis amori?
nec venit in mentem quorum consederis arvis?
hinc Gaetulae urbes, genus insuperabile bello,			40
et Numidae infreni cingunt et inhospita Syrtis ;
hinc deserta siti regio, lateque furentes
Barcaei.   quid bella Tyro surgentia dicam
germanique minas?
dis equidem auspicibus reor et Iunone secunda			45
hunc cursum Iliacas vento tenuisse carinas.
quam tu urbem, soror, hanc cernes, quae surgere regna

coniugio tali! Teucrum comitantibus armis,
Punica se quantis attollet gloria rebus!
tu modo posce deos veniam, sacrisque litatis   50
indulge hospitio, causasque innecte morandi,
dum pelago desaevit hiems et aquosus Orion,
quassataeque rates, dum non tractabile caelum.'
his dictis incensum animum inflammavit amore,
spemque dedit dubiae menti, solvitque pudorem.   55

*Dido seeks, by divination, to learn the attitude of the gods towards
her project. Her passion increases and her preoccupation
with it causes the fortification of Carthage to be suspended.*

Principio delubra adeunt, pacemque per aras
exquirunt : mactant lectas de more bidentes

' PRINCIPIO DELUBRA ADEUNT PACEMQUE PER ARAS
EXQUIRUNT.'
Dido is about to offer sacrifice.
(From the Vatican MS. of Vergil: Fourth Century, A.D.)

legiferae Cereri Phoeboque patrique Lyaeo,
Iunoni ante omnes, cui vincla iugalia curae.
ipsa, tenens dextra pateram, pulcherrima Dido   60
candentis vaccae media inter cornua fundit ;
aut ante ora deum pingues spatiatur ad aras,
instauratque diem donis, pecudumque reclusis
pectoribus inhians spirantia consulit exta.
heu vatum ignarae mentes! quid vota furentem,   65
quid delubra iuvant? est molles flamma medullas
interea, et tacitum vivit sub pectore vulnus.
uritur infelix Dido totaque vagatur
urbe furens, qualis coniecta cerva sagitta,
quam procul incautam nemora inter Cresia fixit   70
pastor agens telis, liquitque volatile ferrum
nescius : illa fuga silvas saltusque peragrat
Dictaeos ; haeret lateri letalis arundo.
nunc media Aenean secum per moenia ducit,
Sidoniasque ostentat opes urbemque paratam ;   75
incipit effari, mediaque in voce resistit :
nunc eadem labente die convivia quaerit,
Iliacosque iterum demens audire labores
exposcit, pendetque iterum narrantis ab ore.
post, ubi digressi, lumenque obscura vicissim   80
luna premit, suadentque cadentia sidera somnos,
sola domo maeret vacua, stratisque relictis
incubat : illum absens absentem auditque videtque ;
aut gremio Ascanium, genitoris imagine capta,
detinet, infandum si fallere possit amorem.   85
non coeptae adsurgunt turres ; non arma iuventus

exercet, portusve aut propugnacula bello
tuta parant : pendent opera interrupta, minaeque
murorum ingentes, aequataque machina caelo.

*Juno suggests to Venus, the mother of Aeneas, that she should
join with her to bring about the marriage.*

Quam simul ac tali persensit peste teneri   90
cara Iovis coniunx nec famam obstare furori,
talibus adgreditur Venerem Saturnia dictis :
' egregiam vero laudem et spolia ampla refertis
tuque puerque tuus, magnum et memorabile nomen,
una dolo divum si femina victa duorum est.   95
nec me adeo fallit, veritam te moenia nostra
suspectas habuisse domos Carthaginis altae.
sed quis erit modus? aut quo nunc certamine tanto?
quin potius pacem aeternam pactosque hymenaeos
exercemus? habes, tota quod mente petisti :   100
ardet amans Dido traxitque per ossa furorem.
communem hunc ergo populum paribusque regamus
auspiciis ; liceat Phrygio servire marito,
dotalesque tuae Tyrios permittere dextrae.'

*Venus is not deceived by Juno's pretence of goodwill towards
herself and her son, but agrees to the proposal if Jupiter's
consent can be won. This Juno pledges herself to obtain,
and plans to bring about the union of Dido and Aeneas.*

Olli—sensit enim simulata mente locutam,   105
quo regnum Italiae Libycas averteret oras—
sic contra est ingressa Venus : ' quis talia demens

abnuat, aut tecum malit contendere bello,
si modo, quod memoras, factum fortuna sequatur?
sed fatis incerta feror, si Iuppiter unam   110
esse velit Tyriis urbem Troiaque profectis,
miscerive probet populos, aut foedera iungi.
tu coniunx ; tibi fas animum temptare precando.
perge ; sequar.'   tum sic excepit regia Iuno :
' mecum erit iste labor. nunc qua ratione. quod
     instat   115
confieri possit, paucis—adverte—docebo.
venatum Aeneas unaque miserrima Dido
in nemus ire parant, ubi primos crastinus ortus
extulerit Titan radiisque retexerit orbem.
hic ego nigrantem commixta grandine nimbum,   120
dum trepidant alae, saltusque indagine cingunt,
desuper infundam, et tonitru caelum omne ciebo.
diffugient comites, et nocte tegentur opaca :
speluncam Dido dux et Troianus eandem
devenient.   adero et, tua si mihi certa voluntas, 125
conubio iungam stabili propriamque dicabo.
hic Hymenaeus erit.'   non adversata petenti
adnuit, atque dolis risit Cytherea repertis.

At dawn, a hunting expedition, in which the queen and Aeneas
     take part, leaves the city for the nearby hills, among which
     the hunt begins.

   Oceanum interea surgens Aurora reliquit.
it portis iubare exorto delecta iuventus :   130
retia rara, plagae, lato venabula ferro,

'AT PUER ASCANIUS MEDIIS IN VALLIBUS ACRI GAUDET EQUO'. Ascanius gallops ahead of Aeneas and Dido; panel from the Low Ham Villa mosaic of the fourth century A.D. (See also cover and pp. 34 and 53 for other panels and reverse of title page for reference).

Massylique ruunt equites, et odora canum vis.
reginam thalamo cunctantem ad limina primi
Poenorum exspectant, ostroque insignis et auro
stat sonipes, ac frena ferox spumantia mandit.   **135**

HUNTING SCENES.
(From a mosaic found at Carthage.)

tandem progreditur magna stipante caterva
Sidoniam picto chlamydem circumdata limbo :
cui pharetra ex auro, crines nodantur in aurum,
aurea purpuream subnectit fibula vestem.
nec non et Phrygii comites et laetus Iulus   **140**
incedunt. ipse ante aiios pulcherrimus omnes
infert se socium Aeneas, atque agmina iungit.
qualis ubi hibernam Lyciam Xanthique fluenta
deserit, ac Delum maternam invisit Apollo,
instauratque choros, mixtique altaria circum   **145**
Cretesque Dryopesque fremunt pictique Agathyrsi :
ipse iugis Cynthi graditur, mollique fluentem

fronde premit crinem fingens, atque implicat auro ;
tela sonant umeris : haud illo segnior ibat
Aeneas ; tantum egregio decus enitet ore.   150
postquam altos ventum in montes atque invia lustra,
ecce ferae saxi deiectae vertice caprae
decurrere iugis ; alia de parte patentes
transmittunt cursu campos atque agmina cervi
pulverulenta fuga glomerant montesque relinquunt.
at puer Ascanius mediis in vallibus acri   155
gaudet equo, iamque hos cursu, iam praeterit illos,
spumantemque dari pecora inter inertia votis
optat aprum, aut fulvum descendere monte leonem.

*A storm arises, as planned by Juno.   Dido and Aeneas take
    shelter in a cave, and become lovers.   This union the queen
    claims as lawful marriage.*

Interea magno misceri murmure caelum   160
incipit ; insequitur commixta grandine nimbus.
et Tyrii comites passim et Troiana iuventus
Dardaniusque nepos Veneris diversa per agros
tecta metu petiere : ruunt de montibus amnes.
speluncam Dido dux et Troianus eandem   165
deveniunt.   prima et Tellus et pronuba Iuno
dant signum : fulsere ignes et conscius aether
conubiis, summoque ulularunt vertice Nymphae.
ille dies primus leti primusque malorum
causa fuit.   neque enim specie famave movetur,   170
nec iam furtivum Dido meditatur amorem :
coniugium vocat ; hoc praetexit nomine culpam.

' SPELUNCAM DIDO DUX ET TROIANUS EANDEM DEVENIUNT.'

The illustration, taken from an MS. of the Aeneid in the Vatican library, shows Dido and Aeneas in the cavern, watched over by two sentries—the one on the left has placed his shield on his head for protection against the rain-storm. Bottom left, are the saddled horses of the lovers.

Rumour, described by Vergil as a winged monster, spreads the news of the union far and wide, and it reaches Iarbas, a native prince whose offer of marriage Dido has previously rejected.

Extemplo Libyae magnas it Fama per urbes,
Fama, malum quā non aliud velocius ullum :

mobilitate viget, viresque adquirit eundo ;   175
parva metu primo ; mox sese attollit in auras,
ingrediturque solo, et caput inter nubila condit.
illam Terra parens, ira inritata deorum,
extremam, ut perhibent, Coeo Enceladoque sororem
progenuit, pedibus celerem et pernicibus alis,   180
monstrum horrendum, ingens, cui quot sunt corpore
     plumae,
tot vigiles oculi subter, mirabile dictu,
tot linguae, totidem ora sonant, tot subrigit aures. ·
nocte volat caeli medio terraeque per umbram
stridens, nec dulci declinat lumina somno.   185
luce sedet custos aut summi culmine tecti,
turribus aut altis, et magnas territat urbes,
tam ficti pravique tenax quam nuntia veri.
haec tum multiplici populos sermone replebat
gaudens, et pariter facta atque infecta canebat :   190
venisse Aenean, Troiano sanguine cretum,
cui se pulchra viro dignetur iungere Dido ;
nunc hiemem inter se luxu, quam longa, fovere,
regnorum immemores turpique cupidine captos.
haec passim dea foeda virum diffundit in ora.   195
protinus ad regem cursus detorquet Iarban,
incenditque animum dictis, atque aggerat iras.

*Iarbas prays for vengeance to his father, Jupiter Ammon,
drawing his attention to Dido's union with Aeneas.*

Hic Hammone satus, rapta Garamantide nympha,
templa Iovi centum latis immania regnis,
centum aras posuit, vigilemque sacraverat ignem,   200

excubias divum aeternas, pecudumque cruore
pingue solum et variis florentia limina sertis.
isque amens animi, et rumore accensus amaro,
dicitur ante aras, media inter numina divum,
multa Iovem manibus supplex orasse supinis':   **205**
'Iuppiter omnipotens, cui nunc Maurusia pictis
gens epulata toris Lenaeum libat honorem,
aspicis haec? an te, genitor, cum fulmina torques,
nequiquam horremus, caecique in nubibus ignes
terrificant animos, et inania murmura miscent?   **210**
femina, quae nostris errans in finibus urbem
exiguam pretio posuit, cui litus arandum,

'MAEONIA MENTUM MITRA CRINEMQUE MADENTEM SUBNIXUS.'

The illustration, from a wall-painting at Pompeii, is of
Paris, and shows clearly the Phrygian cap—Maeonia mitra
—which Iarbas calls effeminate.

cuique loci leges dedimus, conubia nostra
reppulit, ac dominum Aenean in regna recepit.
et nunc ille Paris, cum semiviro comitatu,   **215**
Maeonia mentum mitra crinemque madentem
subnixus, rapto potitur : nos munera templis
quippe tuis ferimus, famamque fovemus inanem.'

*Jupiter sends Mercury to remind Aeneas of his duty to found a
new nation in Italy, and to bid him sail thither without delay.*

Talibus orantem dictis arasque tenentem
audiit Omnipotens, oculosque ad moenia torsit   **220**
regia, et oblitos famae melioris amantes.
tum sic Mercurium adloquitur, ac talia mandat :
' vade age, nate, voca Zephyros, et labere pennis,
Dardaniumque ducem, Tyria Carthagine qui nunc
exspectat, fatisque datas non respicit urbes,   **225**
adloquere, et celeres defer mea dicta per auras.
non illum nobis genetrix pulcherrima talem
promisit, Graiumque ideo bis vindicat armis ;
sed fore, qui gravidam imperiis belloque frementem
Italiam regeret, genus alto a sanguine Teucri —   **230**
proderet, ac totum sub leges mitteret orbem.
si nulla accendit tantarum gloria rerum,
nec super ipse sua molitur laude laborem,
Ascanione pater Romanas invidet arces ?
quid struit? aut qua spe inimica in gente moratur,
nec prolem Ausoniam et Lavinia respicit arva?   **236**
naviget! haec summa est ; hic nostri nuntius esto.'

*Mercury equips himself for flight, and wings his way to
Carthage, where he delivers the message to Aeneas.*

Dixerat. ille patris magni parere parabat
imperio : et primum pedibus talaria nectit
aurea, quae sublimem alis sive aequora supra   **240**
seu terram rapido pariter cum flamine portant.
tum virgam capit ; hac animas ille evocat Orco

pallentes, alias sub Tartara tristia mittit ;
dat somnos adimitque, et lumina morte resignat :
illa fretus agit ventos, et turbida tranat   245
nubila.   iamque volans apicem et latera ardua cernit
Atlantis duri, caelum qui vertice fulcit,
Atlantis, cinctum adsidue cui nubibus atris
piniferum caput et vento pulsatur et imbri ;
nix umeros infusa tegit : tum flumina mento   250
praecipitant senis, et glacie riget horrida barba.
hic primum paribus nitens Cyllenius alis
constitit ; hinc toto praeceps se corpore ad undas
misit, avi similis, quae circum litora, circum
piscosos scopulos, humilis volat aequora iuxta.   255
haud aliter terras inter caelumque volabat
litus harenosum ad Libyae, ventosque secabat
materno veniens ab avo Cyllenia proles.
ut primum alatis tetigit magalia plantis,
Aenean fundantem arces ac tecta novantem   260
conspicit : atque illi stellatus iaspide fulva
ensis erat, Tyrioque ardebat murice laena,
demissa ex umeris, dives quae munera Dido
fecerat, et tenui telas discreverat auro.
continuo invadit : ' tu nunc Carthaginis altae   265
fundamenta locas, pulchramque uxorius urbem
exstruis, heu regni rerumque oblite tuarum?
ipse deum tibi me claro demittit Olympo
regnator, caelum ac terras qui numine torquet ;
ipse haec ferre iubet celeres mandata per auras :   270
quid struis? aut qua spe Libycis teris otia terris?

si te nulla movet tantarum gloria rerum,
nec super ipse tua moliris laude laborem,
Ascanium surgentem et spes heredis Iuli

'MATERNO VENIENS AB AVO CYLLENIA PROLES.'

Mercury, messenger of the gods, is seen with winged sandals,
herald's staff, and wallet.

respice, cui regnum Italiae Romanaque tellus   275
debentur.'   tali Cyllenius ore locutus
mortales visus medio sermone reliquit,
et procul in tenuem ex oculis evanuit auram.

DIDO AND AENEAS WITH VENUS AND CUPID DISGUISED AS ASCANIUS (See *Aeneid* I 657-756); panel from the Low Ham Villa mosaic (see also cover and pp. 25 and 53 for other panels and reverse of title page for reference).

Aeneas obeys, and orders preparations for departure, but is troubled by the necessity to broach the news to the queen.

At vero Aeneas aspectu obmutuit amens,
arrectaeque horrore comae, et vox faucibus haesit.   280
ardet abire fuga, dulcesque relinquere terras,
attonitus tanto monitu imperioque deorum.
heu, quid agat? quo nunc reginam ambire furentem
audeat adfatu? quae prima exordia sumat?
atque animum nunc huc celerem, nunc dividit illuc,
in partesque rapit varias, perque omnia versat.   286

haec alternanti potior sententia visa est :
Mnesthea Sergestumque vocat, fortemque Serestum .
classem aptent taciti, sociosque ad litora cogant ;
arma parent, et quae rebus sit causa novandis   290
dissimulent : sese interea, quando optima Dido
nesciat, et tantos rumpi non speret amores,
temptaturum aditus, et quae mollissima fandi
tempora, quis rebus dexter modus. ocius omnes
imperio laeti parent, et iussa facessunt.   295

> *Dido, however, divines what Aeneas is planning, and with
> many reproaches, begs him to abandon his intention.*

At regina dolos (quis fallere possit amantem?)
praesensit, motusque excepit prima futuros,
omnia tuta timens. eadem impia Fama furenti
detulit armari classem cursumque parari.
saevit inops animi, totamque incensa per urbem   300
bacchatur ; qualis commotis excita sacris
Thyias, ubi audito stimulant trieterica Baccho
orgia, nocturnusque vocat clamore Cithaeron.
tandem his Aenean compellat vocibus ultro :
' dissimulare etiam sperasti, perfide, tantum   305
posse nefas, tacitusque mea decedere terra?
nec te noster amor, nec te data dextera quondam,
nec moritura tenet crudeli funere Dido?
quin etiam hiberno moliris sidere classem,
et mediis properas Aquilonibus ire per altum,   310
crudelis? quid? si non arva aliena domosque
ignotas peteres, et Troia antiqua maneret,

'TANDEM HIS AENEAN COMPELLAT VOCIBUS ULTRO.'
Dido reproaches Aeneas.
(From the Vatican MS. of Vergil.)

Troia per undosum peteretur classibus aequor?
mene fugis? per ego has lacrimas dextramque tuam
    te,—
quando aliud mihi iam miserae nihil ipsa reliqui— 315
per conubia nostra, per inceptos hymenaeos,
si bene quid de te merui, fuit aut tibi quidquam
dulce meum : miserere domus labentis, et istam,
oro, si quis adhuc precibus locus, exue mentem.
te propter Libycae gentes Nomadumque tyranni   320
odere, infensi Tyrii ; te propter eundem
exstinctus pudor, et, qua sola sidera adibam,
fama prior. cui me moribundam deseris, hospes?
hoc solum nomen quoniam de coniuge restat.

quid moror? an mea Pygmalion dum moenia frater
destruat, aut captam ducat Gaetulus Iarbas? 326
saltem si qua mihi de te suscepta fuisset
ante fugam suboles, si quis mihi parvulus aula
luderet Aeneas, qui te tamen ore referret,
non equidem omnino capta ac deserta viderer.' 330

*Aeneas admits his debt to Dido, denies that he had intended to
   steal away secretly, but insists that his destiny lies in Italy,
   and thither, at Mercury's bidding, he must go.*

Dixerat. ille Iovis monitis immota tenebat
lumina, et obnixus curam sub corde premebat.
tandem pauca refert : ' ego te, quae plurima fando
enumerare vales, numquam, regina, negabo
promeritam ; nec me meminisse pigebit Elissae, 335
dum memor ipse mei, dum spiritus hos regit artus.
pro re pauca loquar. neque ego hanc abscondere furto
speravi, ne finge, fugam ; nec coniugis umquam
praetendi taedas, aut haec in foedera veni.
me si fata meis paterentur ducere vitam 340
auspiciis, et sponte mea componere curas,
urbem Troianam primum dulcesque meorum
reliquias colerem ; Priami tecta alta manerent,
et recidiva manu posuissem Pergama victis.
sed nunc Italiam magnam Gryneus Apollo, 345
Italiam Lyciae iussere capessere sortes.
hic amor, haec patria est. si te Carthaginis arces,
Phoenissam, Libycaeque aspectus detinet urbis,
quae tandem, Ausonia Teucros considere terra,

invidia est? et nos fas extera quaerere regna.   350
me patris Anchisae, quotiens umentibus umbris
nox operit terras, quotiens astra ignea surgunt,
admonet in somnis et turbida terret imago ;
me puer Ascanius, capitisque iniuria cari,
quem regno Hesperiae fraudo et fatalibus arvis.   355
nunc etiam interpres divum, Iove missus ab ipso,
(testor utrumque caput) celeres mandata per auras
detulit. ipse deum manifesto in lumine vidi
intrantem muros, vocemque his auribus hausi.
desine meque tuis incendere teque querelis ;   360
Italiam non sponte sequor.'

*Dido bursts out in passionate recriminations, and at last
collapses with the violence of her feelings.*

Talia dicentem iamdudum aversa tuetur,
huc illuc volvens oculos, totumque pererrat
luminibus tacitis, et sic accensa profatur :
' nec tibi diva parens, generis nec Dardanus auctor,
perfide, sed duris genuit te cautibus horrens   366
Caucasus, Hyrcanaeque admorunt ubera tigres.
nam quid dissimulo? aut quae me ad maiora reservo?
num fletu ingemuit nostro? num lumina flexit?
num lacrimas victus dedit, aut miseratus amantem
      est?   370
quae quibus anteferam? iam iam nec maxima Iuno,
nec Saturnius haec oculis pater aspicit aequis.
nusquam tuta fides. eiectum litore, egentem
excepi, et regni demens in parte locavi ;

amissam classem, socios a morte reduxi. 375
heu furiis incensa feror! nunc augur Apollo,
nunc Lyciae sortes, nunc et Iove missus ab ipso
interpres divum fert horrida iussa per auras.
scilicet is superis labor est, ea cura quietos
sollicitat. neque te teneo, neque dicta refello. 380
i, sequere Italiam ventis ; pete regna per undas.
spero equidem mediis, si quid pia numina possunt,
supplicia hausurum scopulis, et nomine Dido
saepe vocaturum. sequar atris ignibus absens ;
et cum frigida mors anima seduxerit artus 385
omnibus umbra locis adero. dabis, improbe, poenas ;
audiam, et haec manes veniet mihi fama sub imos.'
his medium dictis sermonem abrumpit, et auras
aegra fugit, seque ex oculis avertit et aufert,
linquens multa metu cunctantem et multa parantem
dicere. suscipiunt famulae, conlapsaque membra 391
marmoreo referunt thalamo stratisque reponunt.

*Despite his pity for Dido, Aeneas proceeds with the pre-
parations for departure.*

At pius Aeneas, quamquam lenire dolentem
solando cupit et dictis avertere curas, 394
multa gemens, magnoque animum labefactus amore,
iussa tamen divum exsequitur, classemque revisit.
tum vero Teucri incumbunt, et litore celsas
deducunt toto naves. natat uncta carina ;
frondentesque ferunt remos et robora silvis
infabricata, fugae studio. 400

migrantes cernas, totaque ex urbe ruentes ;
ac velut ingentem formicae farris acervum
cum populant, hiemis memores, tectoque reponunt :
it nigrum campis agmen, praedamque per herbas
convectant calle angusto ; pars grandia trudunt   405
obnixae frumenta umeris ; pars agmina cogunt
castigantque moras ; opere omnis semita fervet.

*At the signs of departure Dido's pride is broken and she begs
Anna to plead with Aeneas on her behalf.*

Quis tibi tum, Dido, cernenti talia sensus,
quosve dabas gemitus, cum litora fervere late
prospiceres arce ex summa, totumque videres   410
misceri ante oculos tantis clamoribus aequor?
improbe amor, quid non mortalia pectora cogis?
ire iterum in lacrimas, iterum temptare precando
cogitur, et supplex animos summittere amori,
ne quid inexpertum frustra moritura relinquat.   415
  ' Anna, vides toto properari litore : circum
undique convenere ; vocat iam carbasus auras,
puppibus et laeti nautae imposuere coronas.
hunc ego si potui tantum sperare dolorem,   419
et perferre, soror, potero.   miserae hoc tamen unum
exsequere, Anna, mihi ; solam nam perfidus ille
te colere, arcanos etiam tibi credere sensus ;
sola viri molles aditus et tempora noras.
i, soror, atque hostem supplex adfare superbum :
non ego cum Danais Troianam exscindere gentem   425

Aulide iuravi, classemve ad Pergama misi :
nec patris Anchisae cinerem manesve revelli.
cur mea dicta negat duras demittere in aures ?
quo ruit? extremum hoc miserae det munus amanti :
exspectet facilemque fugam ventosque ferentes.   430
non iam coniugium antiquum, quod prodidit, oro,
nec pulchro ut Latio careat regnumque relinquat :
tempus inane peto, requiem spatiumque furori,
dum mea me victam doceat fortuna dolere.
extremam hanc oro veniam,—miserere sororis ;   435
quam mihi cum dederis, cumulatam morte remittam.'

*Anna's appeals are vain. Aeneas, though far from
unfeeling, is obdurate.*

Talibus orabat, talesque miserrima fletus
fertque refertque soror.   sed nullis ille movetur
fletibus, aut voces ullas tractabilis audit ;
fata obstant, placidasque viri deus obstruit aures.   440
ac velut annoso validam cum robore quercum
Alpini Boreae nunc hinc nunc flatibus illinc
eruere inter se certant ; it stridor, et alte
consternunt terram concusso stipite frondes :
ipsa haeret scopulis, et, quantum vertice ad auras   445
aetherias, tantum radice in Tartara tendit :
haud secus adsiduis hinc atque hinc vocibus heros
tunditur, et magno persentit pectore curas :
mens immota manet ; lacrimae volvuntur inanes.

*Dido now longs for death, and is haunted by terrifying
dreams and omens.*

Tum vero infelix fatis exterrita Dido   450
mortem orat ; taedet caeli convexa tueri.
quo magis inceptum peragat, lucemque relinquat,
vidit, turicremis cum dona imponeret aris,
horrendum dictu, latices nigrescere sacros,
fusaque in obscenum se vertere vina cruorem.   455
hoc visum nulli, non ipsi effata sorori.
praeterea fuit in tectis de marmore templum
coniugis antiqui, miro quod honore colebat,
velleribus niveis et festa fronde revinctum :
hinc exaudiri voces et verba vocantis   460
visa viri, nox cum terras obscura teneret :
solaque culminibus ferali carmine bubo
saepe queri et longas in fletum ducere voces.
multaque praeterea vatum praedicta piorum
terribili monitu horrificant. agit ipse furentem   465
in somnis ferus Aeneas ; semperque relinqui
sola sibi, semper longam incomitata videtur
ire viam, et Tyrios deserta quaerere terra.
Eumenidum veluti demens videt agmina Pentheus,
et solem geminum, et duplices se ostendere
      Thebas ;
aut Agamemnonius scaenis agitatus Orestes   471
armatam facibus matrem et serpentibus atris
cum fugit, ultricesque sedent in limine Dirae.
                                                                .

Dido resolves to destroy herself, but concealing her purpose, bids
  Anna prepare a pyre, pretending that by burning on it all
  that reminds her of Aeneas, she may by magic means be
  cured of her love ; though in reality she plans to die on it
  herself.

Ergo ubi concepit furias evicta dolore
decrevitque mori, tempus secum ipsa modumque   475
exigit, et maestam dictis adgressa sororem
consilium vultu tegit, ac spem fronte serenat :
' inveni, germana, viam—gratare sorori—
quae mihi reddat eum, vel eo me solvat amantem.
oceani finem iuxta solemque cadentem   480
ultimus Aethiopum locus est, ubi maximus Atlas
axem umero torquet stellis ardentibus aptum :
hinc mihi Massylae gentis monstrata sacerdos,
Hesperidum templi custos, epulasque draconi
quae dabat, et sacros servabat in arbore ramos,   485
spargens umida mella soporiferumque papaver.
haec se carminibus promittit solvere mentes
quas velit, ast aliis duras immittere curas ;
sistere aquam fluviis, et vertere sidera retro ;
nocturnosque ciet manes ; mugire videbis   490
sub pedibus terram et descendere montibus ornos.
testor, cara, deos, et te, germana, tuumque
dulce caput, magicas invitam accingier artes.
tu secreta pyram tecto interiore sub auras
erige, et arma viri, thalamo quae fixa reliquit   495
impius, exuviasque omnes, lectumque iugalem,
quo perii, superimponas : abolere nefandi

cuncta viri monimenta iuvat monstratque sacerdos.'
haec effata silet ; pallor simul occupat ora.
non tamen Anna novis praetexere funera sacris   500
germanam credit, nec tantos mente furores
concipit, aut graviora timet quam morte Sychaei.
ergo iussa parat.

Prayers and offerings are made at the completed pyre.

  At regina, pyra penetrali in sede sub auras
erecta, ingenti taedis atque ilice secta,   505
intenditque locum sertis, et fronde coronat
funerea ; super exuvias ensemque relictum
effigiemque toro locat, haud ignara futuri.
stant arae circum, et crines effusa sacerdos
ter centum tonat ore deos, Erebumque Chaosque   510
tergeminamque Hecaten, tria virginis ora Dianae.
sparserat et latices simulatos fontis Averni ;
falcibus et messae ad lunam quaeruntur aënis
pubentes herbae nigri cum lacte veneni ;
quaeritur et nascentis equi de fronte revulsus   515
et matri praereptus amor.
ipsa mola manibusque piis altaria iuxta,
unum exuta pedem vinclis, in veste recincta,
testatur moritura deos et conscia fati
sidera ; tum, si quod non aequo foedere amantes   520
curae numen habet iustumque memorque, precatur.

Dido spends a sleepless night, reviewing o[...]
arguments that had led her to her resolve[...]

Nox erat, et placidum carpebant fess[...]
corpora per terras, silvaeque et saeva quierant
aequora, cum medio volvuntur sidera lapsu,   524
cum tacet omnis ager, pecudes, pictaeque volucres,
quaeque lacus late liquidos, quaeque aspera dumis
rura tenent, somno positae sub nocte silenti
lenibant curas et corda oblita laborum.
at non infelix animi Phoenissa, neque umquam
solvitur in somnos, oculisve aut pectore noctem   530
accipit : ingeminant curae, rursusque resurgens
saevit amor, magnoque irarum fluctuat aestu.
sic adeo insistit, secumque ita corde volutat :
' en, quid ago? rursusne procos inrisa priores
experiar, Nomadumque petam conubia supplex,   535
quos ego sim totiens iam dedignata maritos?
Iliacas igitur classes atque ultima Teucrum
iussa sequar? quiane auxilio iuvat ante levatos,
et bene apud memores veteris stat gratia facti?
quis me autem, fac velle, sinet, ratibusque superbis 540
invisam accipiet? nescis heu, perdita, necdum
Laomedonteae sentis periuria gentis?
quid tum? sola fuga nautas comitabor ovantes?
an Tyriis omnique manu stipata meorum
inferar, et, quos Sidonia vix urbe revelli,   545
rursus agam pelago, et ventis dare vela iubebo?
quin morere, ut merita es, ferroque averte dolorem.

VERGIL

tu lacrimis evicta meis, tu prima furentem
his, germana, malis oneras, atque obicis hosti.
non licuit thalami expertem sine crimine vitam   550
degere, more ferae, tales nec tangere curas!
non servata fides cineri promissa Sychaeo!'
tantos illa suo rumpebat pectore questus.

*Aeneas receives a fresh warning from Mercury, bidding him
    sail at once, for the vengeful Dido may yet destroy his fleet;
    and they put to sea.*

Aeneas celsa in puppi, iam certus eundi,
carpebat somnos, rebus iam rite paratis.   555
huic se forma dei vultu redeuntis eodem
obtulit in somnis, rursusque ita visa monere est,
omnia Mercurio similis, vocemque coloremque
et crines flavos et membra decora iuventa :
' nate dea, potes hoc sub casu ducere somnos?   560
nec, quae te circum stent deinde pericula, cernis,
demens, nec Zephyros audis spirare secundos?
illa dolos dirumque nefas in pectore versat,
certa mori, variosque irarum concitat aestus.
non fugis hinc praeceps, dum praecipitare potestas?
iam mare turbari trabibus, saevasque videbis   566
conlucere faces, iam fervere litora flammis,
si te his attigerit terris Aurora morantem.
heia age, rumpe moras. varium et mutabile semper
femina.' sic fatus nocti se immiscuit atrae.   570
    tum vero Aeneas subitis exterritus umbris
corripit e somno corpus, sociosque fatigat

praecipites: ' vigilate, viri, et considite transtris ;
solvite vela citi. deus aethere missus ab alto
festinare fugam tortosque incidere funes   575
ecce iterum instimulat. sequimur te, sancte deorum,
quisquis es, imperioque iterum paremus ovantes.
adsis o placidusque iuves, et sidera caelo
dextra feras.' dixit, vaginaque eripit ensem
fulmineum, strictoque ferit retinacula ferro.   580
idem omnes simul ardor habet ; rapiuntque ruuntque :
litora deseruere ; latet sub classibus aequor ;
adnixi torquent spumas et caerula verrunt.

*At the sight of the departing fleet, Dido is filled with fury and
despair, and calls down curses on Aeneas and his descendants.*

Et iam prima novo spargebat lumine terras
Tithoni croceum linquens Aurora cubile.   585
regina e speculis ut primum albescere lucem
vidit, et aequatis classem procedere velis,
litoraque et vacuos sensit sine remige portus,
terque quaterque manu pectus percussa decorum
flaventesque abscissa comas, ' pro Iuppiter! ibit   590
hic,' ait, ' et nostris inluserit advena regnis?
non arma expedient, totaque ex urbe sequentur,
deripientque rates alii navalibus? ite,
ferte citi flammas, date vela, impellite remos.
quid loquor? aut ubi sum? quae mentem insania
     mutat?   595
infelix Dido! nunc te facta impia tangunt?
tum decuit, cum sceptra dabas. en dextra fidesque,

quem secum patrios aiunt portare penates,
quem subiisse umeris confectum aetate parentem!
non potui abreptum divellere corpus et undis   600
spargere? non socios, non ipsum absumere ferro
Ascanium, patriisque epulandum ponere mensis?
verum anceps pugnae fuerat fortuna.—fuisset ;
quem metui moritura? faces in castra tulissem,
implessemque foros flammis, natumque patremque   605
cum genere exstinxem, memet super ipsa dedissem.
Sol, qui terrarum flammis opera omnia lustras,
tuque harum interpres curarum et conscia Iuno,
nocturnisque Hecate triviis ululata per urbes,
et Dirae ultrices, et di morientis Elissae,   610

' DIRAE ULTRICES.'

This picture of one of the Furies is from a vase painting.
The figure is seated, but her support is not shown. She
plays with two snakes, and from her brow spring two more.

accipite haec, meritumque malis advertite numen,
et nostras audite preces.   si tangere portus
infandum caput ac terris adnare necesse est,
et sic fata Iovis poscunt, hic terminus haeret :
at bello audacis populi vexatus et armis,   615
finibus extorris, complexu avulsus Iuli,
auxilium imploret, videatque indigna suorum
funera ; nec, cum se sub leges pacis iniquae
tradiderit, regno aut optata luce fruatur,
sed cadat ante diem mediaque inhumatus harena.   620
haec precor; hanc vocem extremam cum sanguine fundo.
tum vos, o Tyrii, stirpem et genus omne futurum
exercete odiis, cinerique haec mittite nostro
munera.   nullus amor populis, nec foedera sunto.
exoriare aliquis nostris ex ossibus ultor,   625
qui face Dardanios ferroque sequare colonos,
nunc, olim, quocumque dabunt se tempore vires.
litora litoribus contraria, fluctibus undas
imprecor, arma armis ; pugnent ipsique nepotesque.'

Sending the nurse of her first husband to fetch Anna, Dido
mounts the pyre, and stabs herself with a sword, the gift to
her of Aeneas.

Haec ait, et partes animum versabat in omnes,   630
invisam quaerens quam primum abrumpere lucem.
tum breviter Barcen nutricem adfata Sychaei ;
namque suam patria antiqua cinis ater habebat :
' Annam, cara mihi nutrix, huc siste sororem ;
dic, corpus properet fluviali spargere lympha.   635

et pecudes secum et monstrata piacula ducat :
sic veniat, tuque ipsa pia tege tempora vitta.
sacra Iovi Stygio, quae rite incepta paravi,
perficere est animus, finemque imponere curis ;
Dardaniique rogum capitis permittere flammae.'   640
sic ait.   illa gradum studio celerabat anili.
at trepida et coeptis immanibus effera Dido,
sanguineam volvens aciem, maculisque trementes
interfusa genas, et pallida morte futura,
interiora domus inrumpit limina, et altos   645
conscendit furibunda rogos, ensemque recludit
Dardanium, non hos quaesitum munus in usus.
hic, postquam Iliacas vestes notumque cubile
conspexit, paulum lacrimis et mente morata,
incubuitque toro, dixitque novissima verba :   650
' dulces exuviae, dum fata deusque sinebant,
accipite hanc animam, meque his exsolvite curis.
vixi, et, quem dederat cursum fortuna, peregi ;
et nunc magna mei sub terras ibit imago.
urbem praeclaram statui ; mea moenia vidi :   655
ulta virum, poenas inimico a fratre recepi :
felix, heu nimium felix, si litora tantum
numquam Dardaniae tetigissent nostra carinae! '
dixit : et os impressa toro, ' moriemur inultae,
sed moriamur,' ait.   ' sic, sic iuvat ire sub umbras.
hauriat hunc oculis ignem crudelis ab alto   661
Dardanus, et nostrae secum ferat omina mortis.'

*Anna hastens to the scene and reproaches her dying sister for her
deceit. Juno seeing Dido's long death agony, sends down
Iris to give a merciful release to her struggling spirit.*

Dixerat : atque illam media inter talia ferro
conlapsam aspiciunt comites, ensemque cruore
spumantem sparsasque manus. it clamor ad alta   665
atria ; concussam bacchatur Fama per urbem.
lamentis gemituque et femineo ululatu
tecta fremunt ; resonat magnis plangoribus aether.
non aliter quam si immissis ruat hostibus omnis
Carthago aut antiqua Tyros, flammaeque furentes   670
culmina perque hominum volvantur perque deorum.
audiit exanimis, trepidoque exterrita cursu
unguibus ora soror foedans et pectora pugnis
per medios ruit, ac morientem nomine clamat :
' hoc illud, germana, fuit? me fraude petebas?   675
hoc rogus iste mihi, hoc ignes araeque parabant?
quid primum deserta querar? comitemne sororem
sprevisti moriens? eadem me ad fata vocasses :
idem ambas ferro dolor atque eadem hora tulisset.
his etiam struxi manibus, patriosque vocavi   680
voce deos, sic te ut posita, crudelis, abessem?
exstinxti te meque, soror, populumque patresque
Sidonios urbemque tuam.   date vulnera lymphis
abluam, et extremus si quis super halitus errat,
ore legam.' sic fata gradus evaserat altos,   685
semianimemque sinu germanam amplexa fovebat
cum gemitu, atque atros siccabat veste cruores.
illa, graves oculos conata attollere, rursus

deficit ; infixum stridit sub pectore vulnus.
ter sese attollens cubitoque adnixa levavit :   690
ter revoluta toro est, oculisque errantibus alto
quaesivit caelo lucem, ingemuitque reperta.

   Tum Iuno omnipotens, longum miserata dolorem
difficilesque obitus, Irim demisit Olympo,
quae luctantem animam nexosque resolveret artus.   695
nam, quia nec fato merita nec morte peribat,
sed misera ante diem, subitoque accensa furore,
nondum illi flavum Proserpina vertice crinem
abstulerat, Stygioque caput damnaverat Orco.
ergo Iris croceis per caelum roscida pennis,   700
mille trahens varios adverso sole colores,
devolat, et supra caput adstitit : ' hunc ego Diti
sacrum iussa fero, teque isto corpore solvo.'
sic ait, et dextra crinem secat.   omnis et una
dilapsus calor, atque in ventos vita recessit.   705

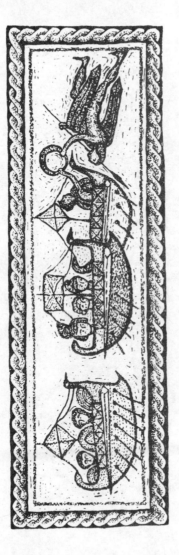

THE TROJAN FLEET: panel from the Low Ham Villa mosaic. (See also cover and pp. 25 and 34 for other panels and reverse of title page for reference); the panel probably shows the fleet arriving in Carthage with Achates taking a gold collar for Dido. (See *Aeneid* I 645-655).

NOTES

Line 1. regina, i.e. Dido, Queen of Carthage, who is entertaining Aeneas, the Trojan prince who is the hero of the poem, at her court. See the story of the Aeneid as told in the Introduction.

gravi cura, abl., depends on saucia, ' troubled ', *lit.*, ' wounded '.

l. 2. vulnus, acc., object of **alit.** The ' wound ' or ' hurt ' is of course the painful love that she is beginning to feel for Aeneas.

caeco. This word, properly ' blind ', ' unseeing ', often means ' unseen ', ' hidden '.

l. 3. viri. ' The hero ' is Aeneas.

animo, dative, ' to her mind '.

l. 4. gentis, ' of his house ' *or* ' family ', i.e. the reigning family of Troy.

pectore is an abl. of place where, very common in poetry without the preposition ' in ' which accompanies it in prose : ' in her breast '.

vultus, nom. pl. So also **verba.,** l. 5.

l. 5. nec placidam, etc. The queen's feelings are so strong as to make sleep difficult.

cura, ' love '.

ll. 6, 7 express in poetic language : ' Day was dawning '.

l. 6. Phoebea lampade. This ' torch of Phoebus ' is the sun, for Phoebus (=Apollo) was the sun-god.

terras, pl. for sg., very common in Latin poetry.

l. 7. Aurora. She was the goddess of the dawn.

polo, abl. of place whence, which would in prose be accompanied by the preposition ' a '.

l. 8. adloquitur. This use of the present tense to describe

past events is carred the 'historic present'. Less common in English than in Latin it is nevertheless familiar enough to us.

male sana. The adverb **male**, going with an adjective, reverses or negatives that adjective's meaning, just as, in French, the opposite of *heureux* is *malheureux*. **male sana** therefore is 'demented', 'distraught'. **Sana** is nom. sing. of the adjective and agrees with the subject ('she', understood) of **adloquitur.**

l. 9. **me suspensam**, *lit.*, 'me anxious', i.e. 'my anxious heart'.

l. 10. To make good sense in English it is necessary to add **est** after **quis** and **qui** before **successit.** The order for translation then is **quis est hic novus hospes qui successit nostris sedibus.**

l. 11. **quem sese ore ferens!**—literally, 'bearing himself what a man in face', i.e. 'what a noble presence he has!'

quam forti pectore et armis, 'with how strong a breast and shoulders' (taking **armis** as from **armi**, not **arma**); i.e. 'what a powerful chest and shoulders are his'.

l. 12. **fides** is subject, **vana** complement, of **est** understood.

genus is complement of **esse**; the subject is **eum** understood. **genus**, usually 'race', is here 'a scion'.

l. 13. **degeneres . . . arguit.** Aeneas shows no fear, and therefore is not **animus degener.**

ll. 13 (from **heu**), 14. 'Alas, harassed by what a fate! What wars endured to the end he sang of!' I.e., 'Alas, by what a fate he has been harassed! What wars he told of, endured to the end.' **Iactatus**=iactatus est.

ll. 15–19. **Sederet** and **pertaesum fuisset** have the meanings usual to the imperfect and pluperfect subjunctives when they occur in the protases ('if' clauses) of conditional sentences: i.e. that something is being assumed which is contrary to the facts of present and past time respectively. Study these examples :

Nisi plueret, domi non essem, 'If it were not raining [*but it is*] I should not be at home ' [*but I am*].

Si rogavisset, locuta esset, ' If he had asked [*but he did not*] she would have spoken ' [*but she did not*].

l. 15. **mihi.** A dative often stands in Latin where English uses a genitive, or a possessive adjective. Translate **mihi** here as if it were **meo** (with **animo**).

animo, ' in my heart '. For the abl. see note on **pectore,** l. 4.

sederet. Translate this word as if it were **esset,** with **fixum** and **immotum** as complements : ' if it were not fixed . . .' The ' it ' anticipates the real subject, which is the clause in l. 16.

l. 16. **ne vellem,** ' that I should not be willing '.

qui, dative of the indefinite pronoun **quis** : ' to any man '.

vinclo iugali, abl. of manner, ' in wed-lock '.

l. 17. **postquam,** ' since '.

deceptam agrees with **me,** which has to be supplied as object to **fefellit.**

l. 18. **pertaesum fuisset,** pluperfect subjunctive of the impersonal verb **pertaedet,** ' it wearies ', which takes an accusative of the person feeling the emotion (here **me** understood) and a genitive of the cause of the emotion (here **thalami** and **taedae**). Thus the line is : ' If I had not been wearied with bridals and marriage '. **Thalamus,** ' bridal-bed ' and **taeda,** ' marriage torch ', both stand for ' marriage '. This figure of speech, in which reference is made to a thing by using instead some word associated with that thing, is known as *metonymy*.

l. 19. **forsan** =forsitan, and the verb it modifies is usually put in the subjunctive.

potui. The verb of a principal clause modified by such ' if' clauses as those in ll. 15, 18, is usually itself in a past tense of the subjunctive. But the indicative is preferred if the verb concerned is one expressing possibility (e.g. **possum**) or obligation. **culpae,** ' weakness '.

l. 20. **fatebor :** supply ' it ' as object.

l. 21. **et sparsos,** etc., *lit.,* ' and since the household god, sprinkled by a brother's slaying ', i.e. ' and since my household gods were bespattered with the blood my brother shed '. The

brother was called Pygmalion and the blood he shed in the
palace chapel was that of Dido's husband Sychaeus.

l. 23. **veteris vestigia flammae.** Dido is reminded by her
feelings towards Aeneas, of those she once entertained for
Sychaeus.

l. 24. ' But I could wish the earth would gape open for me
to its depths ' (**ima**). **optem** is potential subjunctive (equivalent
to a conditional subjunctive with the ' if ' clause suppressed),
and the **tellus dehiscat** clause, which would normally be intro
duced by **ut,** ' that ', depends on it, as does the following clause
pater adigat.

mihi, i.e. to remove her from the temptation to love again.

vel, ' either ', which however may be dropped in translation

prius anticipates the **ante** of l. 27 and is superfluous.

ima, ' most deep ', agrees with **tellus,** and, though an
adjective, does the work of an adverbial phrase modifying
dehiscat.

l. 25. **pater,** i.e. Jupiter, the chief of the gods.

fulmine. The thunderbolt was the special weapon of
Jupiter.

ad umbras. Dido means the underworld, Hades.

l. 26. **Erebi.** Erebus was one of the names for Hades.

l. 27. Treat **antequam,** here separated, as one word, ' before '.

l. 28. **ille,** i.e. Sychaeus.

l. 29. **habeat** and **servet** are subjunctives expressing wishes,
' let him ' or ' may he, have ', etc.

sepulchro, local abl. without preposition. **Cf. note on**
pectore, l. 4.

l. 31. **o luce,** etc.   ' O thou dearer to thy sister than life '.
luce is abl. of comparison, and **sorori** is properly dative of the
agent, ' by thy sister ', going with the participle **dilecta,**
' beloved '.   In the word **sorori** Anna is, of course, referring
to herself.   **Lux,** properly ' light ', is not uncommon in the
meaning ' life '.

solane. The enclitic **ne** as usual marks the question.

l. 32. carpēre = carpěris, 2nd sg. fut. ind. pass., ' will you wear yourself away '—the passive, as very often, being equal to the active voice + reflexive pronoun, **te carpes.** The proper meaning of **carpo** is ' pluck ', from which the notion of ' fretting' is an easy extension.

perpetua. The suggestion is not of course that **iuventa** will for Dido be ' everlasting ', but that the lonely grief and fretting will continue throughout her youth. l. 32 may then be rendered : ' Will you wear yourself away, grieving in solitude (**sola**) all your youth? '

l. 33. noris is a 'syncopated'', i.e. shortened, form of noveris, 2nd sg. fut. perf. ind. act. of **nosco.** Syncopation involves the disappearance of a **v**, and sometimes of the vowel that follows it. Compare **iit** for **ivit, amasse** for **amavisse.** The meaning of **nosco,** ' get to know ', gives to the perfect **novi** a present meaning, ' I know ' ; consequently the future perfect will be equivalent to a future simple. **Nec . . . noris,** therefore, is ' and will you not know? '

l. 34. Begin with **credis** ; then the construction is acc. and infin., with **cinerem** and **manes** subjects of **curare,** and **id** its object : ' Do you believe that ashes, or buried shades, care for that? ' ' That ', **id,** is the solitary grieving of l. 32, an exhibition of constancy which Anna says can have no effect upon the dead. ' Buried shades ' is Vergilian language for ' spirits of the dead '.

l. 35. esto, *lit.*, ' let it be ' (3rd sg. imperative of **sum**) = ' granted that . . .'

aegram agrees with **te** understood, *lit.*, ' (thee) sick '. Translate ' thy sick heart '.

mariti. By this word (= ' husbands ') Anna means of course ' would-be husbands ', i.e. ' suitors '.

l. 36. Libyae, locative, and **Tyro,** abl. of place where, ' in Africa ', ' at Tyre '. Tyre was the Phoenician city which Dido left to found Carthage.

despectus, supply **est.** The influence of **esto** still persists. Render ' though Iarbas be scorned '. Iarbas, who is described as wooing Dido unsuccessfully, was a native African prince.

l. 37. **ductores**, nominative to **despecti sunt**, easily understood from despectus (est) of l. 36.

terra triumphis dives, ' land rich in triumphs '. The phrase is in apposition to Africa, which is so called as being the home of martial races.

l. 38. **placitone**. See note on **solane**, l. 32. Placito is ' favoured '. Pugnabis, with its dative (of disadvantage) expressing ' against ', may. be translated ' will you resist '.

l. 39. ' And does it not enter thy mind in whose lands thou hast settled? ' Anna means that a marriage with Aeneas is politic, as giving Dido needed support against possible enemies. **Consederis** is subjunctive in the indirect question introduced by **quorum**, the whole clause being the subject of **venit**. **Arvis** is abl. of place where without preposition—cf. **pectore**, l. 4, **Tyro**, l. 36, etc.

l. 40. **hinc** =' on this side ', and is balanced by a second **hinc**, l. 42 =' on that '.

Gaetulae. The Gaetulians were an African tribe of the interior.

genus is in apposition to **urbes**, though of course it refers rather to the population of the cities.

insuperabile. Parse this carefully.

bello, ' in war ', is ablative of respect. Cf. **hostes numero erant superiores**, ' the enemy were superior in numbers '.

l. 41. **Numidae**. The Numidians were the most immediate African neighbours of Carthage.

infreni, ' riding without bridles ', the adjective being chosen to suggest the excellence of their horsemanship.

cingunt governs **te** understood.

Syrtis. The Syrtis was a vast, dangerous sand-bank off the African coast.

l. 42. **siti**, abl. of cause modifying **deserta**, ' deserted owing to thirst '. Translate the whole phrase 'a thirsty desert region '. **Regio** is subject to **est**, ' there is ', understood.

l. 43. **Barcaei.** There was a city of N. Africa called Barce.

quid dicam, ' why should I tell of '—meaning, surely those are enemies enough, without mentioning these others. **dicam** is *deliberative* subjunctive.

surgentia, i.e. ' threatening '.

l. 44. **germani.** Dido's brother, described as threatening war, is that Pygmalion who had slain her husband Sychaeus. See note, l. 21.

ll. 45, 46. ' For my part I think that under the guidance of the gods and with Juno's favour the Trojan ships held this course with the wind '. **carinas tenuisse** is acc. and infin., object of **reor**. **Dis auspicibus** and **Iunone secunda** are abl. absolutes, ' with the gods (as) guides and Juno favouring '. ' This course ' is the course to Africa. Juno might be supposed to favour Aeneas's remaining in Africa as the husband of Dido, since this would involve his abandonment of his destiny, namely the re-establishment on Italian soil of the Trojan people, to whom Juno was an implacable enemy.

carinas. carina, literally ' keel ', is very often used in poetry for ' ship ', just as in English we have such expressions as ' a fleet of twenty sail '. This figure of speech, the use of a word denoting part of a thing, to express the thing itself is called *synecdoche*.

l. 47. **surgere** has to be taken with both halves of the sentence, and in slightly different senses : ' What a city shall you see this *grow into*, what an empire *spring* from such a marriage! ' **coniugio tali** may be either a variety of abl. of place whence without preposition (cf. **polo**, l. 7) or abl. abs., ' the marriage (being) such '.

ll. 48, 49. **Teucrum**, etc. ' Attended by the might of the Trojans, with what great fortunes will Punic glory rise! ' **Teucrum** is gen. pl., for the more usual **Teucrorum**. **comitantibus armis**, ' with the arms attending ' is abl. abs. ' Rise ', literally ' raise itself ' (**se attollet**).

l. 50. deos veniam. posco, like other Latin verbs of asking, can take two accusatives ; in English veniam will be ' for pardon '. Anna seems to suggest that Dido's rejection of love has earned the ill will of the gods.

sacris litatis, abl. abs.

l. 51. **causas innecte morandi,** *lit.,* ' weave reasons of delaying ', i.e. ' seek excuses for him (Aeneas) to tarry '.

l. 52. **pelago,** ' upon the sea ' ; ' local ' ablative, cf. **pectore,** l. 4.

Orion, a constellation associated with bad weather.

l. 53. **quassatae,** sc. **sunt.** The present tense is required by the sense, and should be substituted.

non tractabile : supply **est.**

l. 54. **incensum,** ' (already) on fire '.

l. 56. **pacem per aras exquirunt,** *lit.,* ' seek peace amid the altars ', i.e. ' seek to win favour at every altar '—to placate, that is, each of the various divinities with offerings.

l. 57. **de more,** ' according to custom ', i.e. with proper observance of religious ceremonial.

l. 58. **Cereri.** Ceres was the goddess of agriculture, and is called **legifera** as the patroness of civilization and law.

Phoebo. Phoebus, also called Apollo, was the god of the sun, of prophecy and poetry, and of archery.

Lyaeo. Lyaeus, Greek for ' he who frees from care ', was a title of Bacchus, the god of the vine. The addition **pater** suggests reverence and might be used with the name of any god.

l. 59. **cui,** etc., *lit.,* ' to whom marriage bonds (are) for a care ', i.e. ' in whose care are the ties of wedlock '. **Curae** is predicative dative, i.e. a dative, used where English prefers a nominative, as the complement of the verb **sum.** The use is restricted to abstract nouns. For another example cf. **avidum mare est exitio nautis,** ' the greedy sea is (for) a destruction to sailors '.

l. 60. **dextra,** *lit.,* ' with her right (hand) '. In English we prefer ' in '. **Dextra,** and **laeva** or **sinistra** (=' left ') are all very often used for right and left *hand* respectively.

l. 61. **fundit.** The object is **eam (pateram),** understood, or rather the wine contained in it.

media inter cornua, *lit.,* ' between the mid horns ' =' midway between the horns '.

l. 62. **ora deum,** ' the faces of the gods ', i.e. of their images. **deum** is gen. pl.

pingues, ' rich ', no doubt so called because of the rich gifts heaped on them.

l. 63. **pecudum reclusis pectoribus,** ' laying open the breasts of beasts ', i.e. in order to inspect the entrails for omens, as was the custom of Roman religion. **reclusis pectoribus** is abl. abs. The final syllable of **pectoribus** is here counted long, as it regularly was in older Latin.

l. 64. **inhians,** *lit.,* ' gaping ', i.e. ' eagerly '.

spirantia, ' breathing ', i.e. ' still pulsing with life '.

consulit, i.e. to look for omens.

l. 65. **quid vota . . . iuvant.** *Lit.,* ' What do vows, what do temples help (her), lovesick? ' I.e. ' Of what use to her, in the madness of love, are vows and shrines.' **Quid** is an adverbial, not an objective accusative. **Furentem** agrees with **eam,** understood.

l. 66. **est,** 3rd sg. pres. indic. act. of edo, ' eat '.

l. 67. **tacitum,** *lit.,* ' silent ', ' unheard '; perhaps the meaning is rather ' unseen '.

vulnus, and **flamma** of l. 66, mean, of course, the ' flame ' and the ' wound ' of her passion for Aeneas.

l. 68. **tota urbe,** ' over all the city '. Phrases of ' place ' which include the word **totus** are usually found, even in prose, without prepositions.

l. 69. **qualis . . . sagitta,** ' like a hind struck by an arrow ', *lit.,* ' an arrow having been shot ', abl. abs.

l. 70. **quam** is the object, **pastor** (l. 71) the subject, of **fixit. procul,** ' *from* afar '.

Cresia. This adjective was chosen perhaps because Crete was an island famous for its archers.

l. 71. **agens,** ' hunting (it) '.

liquit, ' has left (in her) '.

volatile ferrum. The ' winged steel ' is, of course, the shepherd's arrow.

l. 72. **nescius,** *lit.,* ' unaware '. Translate ' though he knows it not '.

illa, i.e. the hind.

fuga, abl., ' in flight '.

l. 73. **lateri,** dat. =' in its flank '.

l. 74. **Aenean,** Greek acc. sg.

moenia, *lit.,* ' walls '. Translate ' buildings '.

l. 75. **Sidonias.** The wealth is called ' Sidonian ' because Sidon was a city of the Phoenicians, who colonized Carthage.

paratam, ' ready (for habitation) '.

l. 76. **voce,** *lit.,* ' voice '; here ' speech ' or ' utterance '.

l. 77. **labente die,** abl. abs., ' the day gliding on ', i.e. ' as the day grows old '. The Roman hour for dining was usually the ninth, that is, well into the afternoon.

eadem convivia quaerit, ' seeks the same company ', i.e. that of Aeneas. **convivia** is an instance of the use of the plural for the singular, which, like the converse, is a very common licence in Latin poetry.

l. 78. **Iliacos labores.** These ' tribulations of Troy ' are the capture and destruction of the city, the story of which Aeneas had already once told to Dido (Book II).

demens, ' foolishly ', because she thereby makes worse her love-sickness. The use of adjectives where English prefers adverbs is common.

l. 79. **narrantis ab ore,** ' from the narrator's mouth ' =' on his lips as he tells his tale '.

l. 80. **post,** adverb, ' afterwards '.

digressi, sc. sunt, ' they (i.e. Dido and Aeneas) have parted '.

obscura vicissim, ' darkening in her turn '.   The moon is
setting, as, the evening before, the sun had done.   The banquet
and Aeneas' story that followed it, had lasted almost till
morning.   This is borne out by ' the setting stars advise
repose ', l. 81.

l. 81. **premit,** ' veils '.

somnos, pl. for sg.   Cf. note on **convivia,** l. 77.

l. 82. **maeret.**   The subject is Dido.

vacua goes with **domo,** as scansion shows.   **domo** and **stratis**
are abls. of the kind explained in the note on **pectore,** l. 4.

l. 83.   **illum,** i.e. Aeneas.

absens absentem.   Translate ' though he is not with her '.
The repetition of the word, **absens** agreeing with the subject
understood, **absentem** with the object, **illum,** emphasizes the
idea of their separation.

l. 84. **gremio,** ' in her lap '.   Cf. note on **pectore,** l. 4.

Ascanium.   This was the name of the young son of Aeneas.
He is also called Iulus.

genitoris imagine capta, ' captivated by his father's features ',
which she sees reproduced in the child's face.

l. 85. **si possit,** ' in the hope that she may be able '.

fallere.   Dido hopes to ease her passion by the contempla-
tion of features like those of Aeneas.

ll. 86–89.   Dido's preoccupation with her personal problem
brings to a standstill the building of her city of Carthage.

l. 86. **non** goes with **adsurgunt.**

l. 87. **portusve.**   The enclitic **-ve** means ' or '.   **bello tuta,**
' safe in war ', i.e. ' proof against foes '.   **bello** is like **pectore,**
l. 4.

l. 88. **non parant.**   The subject is ' they '—the men of the
city.

minae murorum ingentes, *lit.,* ' great threats of walls ',
Vergilian expression for ' great, frowning walls '.   Elsewhere
he has **strata viarum** for ' paved streets ', ' **lapsus rotarum** for
' gliding wheels '.

l. 89. machina. Doubtless some form of crane.

l. 90. quam teneri, ' that she was possessed ', acc. and infin. depending on **persensit.** ' She ' is Dido. It is very common in Latin to begin a sentence with a relative pronoun, referring to some person or thing mentioned in a previous sentence. This is rare in English, and we must usually substitute the appropriate personal or demonstrative pronoun. Hence ' she ' is substituted here for the literal ' whom '.

peste. The ' sickness ' of course is the queen's love for Aeneas.

l. 91. cara Iovis coniunx, i.e. Juno.

nec ... furori, ' and that (regard-for-) her-reputation (**famam**) did not withstand her madness ', still acc. and infin. depending on **persensit.** The sense is that Dido allowed no fear of what the world might say to restrain her.

l. 92. talibus dictis, ' with such words *as these* '.

ll. 93–95. These lines are ironical, Juno's real meaning being contrary to what she actually says.

l. 93. refertis. The subject is tuque puerque tuus, ' you and your boy '. The first -que, ' both ', need not be translated. The boy, of course, is Cupid.

l. 95. divum, gen. pl. of **divus.** The ' two gods ' are Venus and Cupid, the ' one woman ' Dido.

l. 96. nec me fallit te, ' nor does it escape me that you ... '

te habuisse is acc. and infin., subject to **fallit.**

veritam, ' fearing ', agrees with **te.** The perfect participles of deponent verbs are often used with a present meaning.

moenia nostra. Juno is referring to the walls of Carthage, and calls them ' our walls ' because she favoured that city particularly. The plural **noster** instead of **meus** is very common, and quite appropriate in the mouth of a goddess.

l. 97. suspectas habuisse, ' have held suspect ', i.e. ' in suspicion '. Venus, with her ambition that Aeneas shall found a city—Rome—in Italy, is charged by Juno with a jealous suspicion of Juno's own city of Carthage.

l. 98. aut quo . . . certamine tanto, *lit.*, ' or to what end now with so much contention? ' i.e. ' or what now boots such contention '. Juno guilefully suggests that Venus's resistance to Juno's own plans is needless—for they can, she says, join forces.

l. 100. exercemus, ' favour '.

quod =id quod, ' that which ', ' what '. This omission of a demonstrative antecedent is very common.

petisti =petivisti. This is called a syncopated form, and occurs through the dropping of a **v**, and sometimes, as here, of a following vowel as well. Cf. **amarunt** for amaverunt.

l. 101. ardet amans, ' is afire loving ' =' is aflame with love '.

traxitque, etc., *lit.*, ' and has drawn the madness through her bones ', i.e. ' and has suffered its madness to fill her body '.

l. 102. communem. Translate this adjective, which is predicative and emphatic, by an adverbial phrase, ' in common '.

paribus auspiciis, ' with equal authority ' ; i.e. Juno proposes that she and Venus shall govern the suggested union of peoples as equals. **Auspicium** means ' divination by the flight of birds ', and the meaning ' authority ' derives from the fact that such divination was the privilege of Roman magistrates.

regamus, ' let us rule '. This use of the subjunctive, expressing an exhortation or command in the 1st person, is called hortative.

l. 103. liceat servire, ' let her be a slave '. **liceat,** from the impersonal verb **licet,** ' it is allowed ', is a jussive subjunctive, i.e. a subjunctive expressing a command in the 3rd, and more rarely the 2nd person.

Phrygio marito, i.e. Aeneas, since **Phrygius** =' Trojan '.

l. 104. dotales agrees with **Tyrios** and is to be translated ' as her dowry '.

dextrae, *lit.*, ' right hand ', may be translated ' power '.

l. 105. Olli is an old form of **illi** (dat. sg. fem.).

sensit, etc. The line is a little condensed, and **eam** (= Juno) and **esse,** with **locutam,** are to be understood.

(eam) locutam (esse) is acc. and infin., dependent on **sensit.**

mens may be rendered here by ' purpose '.

l. 106. **quo** is here equal to **ut** final : ' in order that '.

oras, for **ad oras.** This is called the accusative of the goal of motion and is a poetic construction.

The meaning of ll. 105, 106 is that Venus sees through Juno's pretence of friendship and divines that it conceals a real intention to frustrate the founding in Italy of a revived Trojan power by Aeneas.

contra, adverb.

l. 107. **est ingressa,** for the more usual order **ingressa est.**

ll. 107–108. **quis . . . abnuat,** ' who would be so mad as to refuse such things '.

l. 108. **malit,** similarly, ' would prefer '. The subjunctives are conditional.

bello, ' in war '.

l. 109. **factum,** ' the course ', *lit.,* ' deed '. **sequatur,** ' should attend ', i.e. ' favour '. Venus suggests a doubt as to whether destiny will approve the course which Juno proposes.

l. 110. **sed . . . feror,** ' but the fates keep me in doubt ', *lit.,* ' I am carried, uncertain, by the fates '.

si, instead of the regular **num,** introducing an indirect question, with its verbs, **velit, probet,** in the subjunctive as usual.

l. 111. **esse,** ' that there should be '.

Tyriis, profectis, datives, ' for . . .' **Troiâque profectis,** ' and for those that set out from Troy ', i.e. for Aeneas and his Trojans. **profectis** is dat. pl. masc. of the perf. partic.

l. 112. **probet,** still dependent on **si,** l. 110, ' or (-ve) whether he approves '.

populos, i.e. the Tyrian and Trojan peoples.

iungi, ' be made '. **iungo,** not **facio,** is commonly used in

Latin **where** English prefers ' make ', in **cases** where the making involves a union or joining of forces, **as** with such words as **foedus, societas,** etc.

l. 113. **tu coniunx,** supply **es eius. fas,** sc. **est.**

temptare, ' to probe ', i.e. seek to discover what is in Juppiter's mind.

precando, ' with entreaty ', *lit.,* ' by entreating ', abl. of the gerund of **precor.**

l. 115. **mecum,** ' mine ', *lit.,* ' with me '.

ll. 115, 116. Order for translation is : Nunc **adverte** : paucis (verbis) docebo qua ratione (id) quod instat possit confieri. **paucis,** agreeing with **verbis** understood, ' in few words '. **quod instat,** ' that which presses ', i.e. ' the pressing task '. **confieri** for **confici,** pres. infin. pass. **possit,** subjunctive in the indirect question dependent on **qua ratione. docebo,** understand **te as** object.

l. 117. **venatum,** ' a-hunting ' ; the supine in -**m** (really **an** acc., expressing the goal of action, of a verbal noun) denotes purpose after the verb of motion, **ire.** This acc. is similar to the acc. of place names after similar verbs, e.g. **Romam proficisci,** ' to set out for Rome '.

unaque, ' and together (with him) '. **una** is the adverb.

l 118. **ortus,** acc. pl.

l. 119. **extulerit,** fut. perf., where English prefers the perfect. ' Shall have lifted his first risings ' =' has newly risen ' simply.

Titan, Vergilian for ' the sun ', which, according to a Greek myth, was the son of the Titan, or giant, Hyperion. Thus **ll.** 118, 119 from **ubi** onwards mean merely ' at dawn tomorrow ', expressed in a poetic manner.

retexerit, also fut. perfect. Note the force of **re-,** here = to English **un-, and** compare **recludo,** ' open ', from **claudo,** ' shut '.

l. 120. **commixta grandine,** ' with hail mingled '. We should expect **commixtum grandine,** ' mingled with hail ', (with **commixtum** qualifying **nimbum).**

nimbum is object of **infundam**, l. 122.

l. 121. **dum trepidant alae.** The sense of these words is doubtful. It is, however, simplest to take **ala** in its military meaning of ' squadron ', in which case the translation is : ' while the mounted hunters hasten '.

saltus, acc. pl.

l. 124. **speluncam**, an acc. of the goal of motion—**ad speluncam** in prose. Cf. **oras**, l. 106.

l. 125. **tua si**, etc., ' if your goodwill (is) assured for me ', i.e. ' if I am assured of your goodwill '.

l. 126. **iungam.** Supply **eos** as object.

propriamque dicabo, ' and will make (her) his own '.

l. 127. **non adversata petenti**, ' not opposing (her) asking ', i.e. ' without opposing her request '. **petenti** is of course dat. sg. fem. of the present participle, and agrees with **ei**, standing for Juno, understood, and governed by **adversata**.

l. 128. **adnuit.** The subject is Cytherea.

Cytherēa, i.e. Venus, because the island of Cythera was the site of a famous temple to the goddess.

dolis repertis, abl. abs., ' her wiles having been detected ', i.e ' for she had detected her deceit '.

l. 130. **portis**, abl. of route, ' through the gates '.

iubare exorto, abl. abs., best rendered here by a ' when ' clause.

iuventus, collective ; a plural, ' youths ', is more natural in English. **delecta**, ' chosen ' to attend on the queen and her guest—for their nobility of birth and prowess in the chase, no doubt.

l. 131. To the nominatives **retia, plagae, venabula** supply **sunt**, ' there are '. **retia, plagae** : possibly two different types of hunting net. Nets were used by ancient huntsmen to prevent game breaking out of the area chosen for the beat, and were often furnished with feathers dyed in bright colours, the fluttering of which terrified the quarry and prevented attempts at escape.

lato ferro, ' with broad iron ', i.e. ' broad-bladed '. This is the ablative of description, which invariably consists of noun and adjective.

l. 132. odora canum vis, ' the keen-scented strength of hounds ', a poetic expression for ' powerful, keen-scented hounds '.

l. 133. thalamo, ' *in* her chamber '—abl. of place where without preposition, cf. note on pectore, l. 4. ad, ' near '. thalamo and ad limina both go closely with cunctantem, ' lingering '.

primi is used as a noun, ' the first ', i.e., ' leading, men '.

l. 134. ostro et auro, ' *in* purple and gold '—the royal trappings make the queen's mount conspicuous.

l. 135. sonipes, by derivation ' clatter-foot ', =' horse '.

ferox, adj. for adv., ' spiritedly '.

frena, pl. for sg.—very common in verse. Cf. convivia and note, l. 77.

l. 136. progreditur, the subject is Dido.

magna stipante caterva, abl. abs., ' with a great throng pressing (about her) '.

l. 137. circumdata, ' wearing '. The participle is an example of a construction not uncommon among the Roman poets, by which the passive voice is used as an equivalent for the active+a reflexive pronoun in the dative case. This use derives from Greek, which has a third voice, for the most part identical in form with the passive, which is employed to express action done to or for oneself. This voice is called ' middle ', and circumdata, which means literally ' having put round herself ', is an instance of the ' middle use of the passive voice '. Note that this middle voice can take a direct object, in this case chlamydem.

l. 138. cui, a dative where a genitive, cuius, would be expected. Translate ' her ', and take it with pharetra, crines and vestem. Cf. note on mihi, l. 15, and for the use of the relative, see note on quam, l. 90.

pharetra is subject to est understood.

ex auro, ' of gold '.

nodantur in aurum, *lit.*, ' are knotted into gold ', i.e. ' are bound with golden bands '.

l. 140. **nec non et.** The negatives **nec** and **non** cancel out, leaving only the conjunctional part of **nec**, meaning ' and '. The **et** that follows is ' also '. The use of **nec non** gives Vergil a spondaic equivalent for **et, ac, atque**.

laetus, because he is going hunting.

l. 142. **infert se socium**, *lit.*, ' carries himself onwards (as) her companion ', i.e. ' comes to her side '.

agmina, ' the (two) parties ', i.e. his own and the queen's. Aeneas, riding over to place himself at the queen's side, is followed by his Trojan retainers, and so the two parties become one.

ll. 143–150. This long simile compares Aeneas to the sun-god Apollo in beauty and swiftness of movement. Begin with the words **qualis ubi Apollo**, ' even as Apollo when he . . .'

l. 143. **Lyciam.** In this part of Asia Minor Apollo had a famous temple at Patara.

Xanthi, the name of a river in Lycia.

l. 144. **Delum maternam.** Delos is called ' his mother's ' because Leto hid upon that island from the jealous anger of Hera, and gave birth to Apollo there.

l. 145. **altaria** is governed by **circum**.

l. 146. **Dryopes, Agathyrsi**, names of ancient people, living in Thessaly and Scythia respectively.

l. 147. **iugis**, abl. of place where. Cf. **pectore** and note, l. 4.

Cynthi. Cynthus was a mountain in the island of Delos.

l. 148. **fingens, premit :** translate as two finite verbs, ' dresses his flowing locks and confines them '. **fingo** is used to describe the process of *ordering* his locks, **premo** that of giving the resultant order permanence by *binding* them with a garland, while **implicat auro** means the final securing of hair and garland in place with a band of gold.

l. 149. **tela sonant umeris.** As he strides swiftly along the heights of the mountain, the quiver full of arrows rattles upon his back. **umeris,** same abl. as iugis, l. 147.

segnior, adj. for adv. Cf. **ferox,** l. 135.

illo, abl. of comparison, ' than he '. **ille** is Apollo.

l. 150. **ore,** abl. of place whence. Cf. **polo** and note, **l. 7.**

l. 151. **Postquam ventum,** supply **est,** ' when it was come ' =' when they came '. This is the impersonal passive construction, common in Latin, a familiar example being the Caesarian **ab utrisque acriter pugnatum est,** ' both sides fought fiercely '.

l. 152. **deiectae.** The passive in Latin is very often equivalent to the active used reflexively. Thus **deiectae** here, *lit.,* ' having been thrown down ' =' having thrown themselves down ', ' having leapt '.

l. 153. **decurrēre,** 3rd pl. perf. indic. act., not pres. infin., **as** the scansion shows.

iugis, abl. of route, ' along . . .'

l. 154. **cursu,** *lit.,* ' by running ', i.e. ' at speed '.

ll. 154, 155. **agmina . . . pulverulenta fuga glomerant,** *lit.,* ' gather their dusty bands in flight ', i.e. ' herd together in flight, raising clouds of dust '.

l. 157. **hos, illos** ; either groups of hunters, or herds of deer. **cursu,** ' at full gallop '.

ll. 158, 159. ' And prays that, among the timid herds, a foaming wild-boar be granted to his desires, or that a tawny lion should descend from the mountain '. **aprum dari,** acc. and infin. after **opto.**

spumantem, ' foaming ', of course, with rage.

l. 160. **magno misceri murmure,** *lit.,* ' to be mingled with a great murmur ', i.e. ' to fill with a deep, confused rumbling '. Vergil is fond of using **misceo** to suggest confusion. Notice the alliteration in the phrase, intended to imitate the sound of distant thunder. This is an instance of what is called *onomatopoeia*, the matching of sound to sense. L. 160, of course, describes the onset of the storm planned by Juno, l. 120.

l. 161. **commixta grandine nimbus.** See l. 120 and note.

l. 162. **iuventus.** See note on this word, l. 130.

l. 163. **Dardanius nepos Veneris.** The reference is to Ascanius (Iulus). His father, Aeneas, was the son of Venus and the Trojan prince Anchises.

l. 165. **speluncam** for **ad speluncam**, acc. of the goal of motion. Cf. note on **oras**, l. 106.

ll. 166–168. Aeneas and the queen are united in love. These lines declare poetically that Heaven (represented by Juno) and Mother Earth (Tellus—a personification) sanction this union, the sky shows its awareness by flashes of lightning, and the mountain nymphs, demi-goddesses, greet it with shrill outcry.

l. 166. **prima**, adj. for adv. **pronuba**, ' (as) bride's attendant '. Note this common use of simple apposition where English prefers to employ ' as '.

l. 167. **fulsere**, short form of the 3rd pl. perf. ind. act. of **fulgeo**. Cf. **petiere**, l. 164.

ignes, the lightnings of course. **conscius**, ' confederate '. The **aether**, ' upper air ', ' sky ', *shares the knowledge*—the roots of **conscius** being **cum** and **scio**.

l. 168. **conubiis**, ' at their union '. The abl. may be that of cause, or of time when.

ululurunt, 3rd pl. perf. act. This is called a syncopated (' cut short ') form, standing as it does for **ululaverunt**. These forms occur through the dropping of a **v**, and sometimes as here, of the following vowel. A more familiar example is **petiere** = **petiverunt**, l. 164.

vertice, abl. of place where without preposition, ' on . . .'. Cf. **pectore**, l. 4.

l. 169. ' That was the first day of death, that day was first the cause of evil.' The ' death ' is doubtless the queen's, and by the 'evils' Vergil probably means the bitter wars between Rome and Carthage, cities founded by Aeneas and Dido respectively. malorum is neut. pl.

l. 170. specie famave, ' by (thoughts of) appearances or reputation ', i.e. she does not care how her union with Aeneas will appear to others nor what they will say of it and her.

movetur. The subject of this verb, as of meditatur, is Dido.

l. 172. coniugium vocat, ' she calls (it) marriage '. The ' it ' is of course their union.

l. 174. qua, abl. of comparison, ' than which '. malum aliud ullum is the subject, velocius the complement of est understood. non ullum =nullum, ' no '.

l. 175. mobilitate viget, ' her power lies in her swiftness ', *lit.*, ' she flourishes owing to her quickness '. mobilitate is abl. of cause.

eundo, abl. of the gerund, ' by going ', i.e. ' as she goes '.

l. 176. parva metu primo, ' at first, in her timidity, (she is) small '. metu is abl. of cause, like mobilitate in the previous line. Rumour is described by Vergil as a puny fearful creature who swells into a monster as she sweeps across the world.

l. 177. solo. Same abl. as pectore, l. 4; ' upon...';

l. 178. illam =Famam ; it is the object, and Terra parens is the subject, of progenuit, l. 180. ira inritata deorum, ' provoked by anger against the gods '. The fact that relationships between one noun and another can only be expressed in Latin by the genitive case leads to numerous difficult genitives, not readily classifiable. deorum here, however, is not far from the objective gen., of which a typical example is amor patris, ' love for one's father '.

l. 179. ' A last sister, as they tell, to C. and E.,' i.e. ' youngest sister of ', etc. sororem is in apposition to illam, l. 178.

perhibent. Notice this verb particularly. You would hardly guess its meaning.

Coeus was a Titan, and Enceladus a Giant. Both Titans and Giants were monstrous offspring of Earth.

l. 180. **pedibus celerem**, ' speedy of foot '. **pedibus is abl.** of respect.

ll. 181-183. ' A dreadful monster, huge, who beneath every feather on her body, strange to tell, has a watchful eye, speaking tongue and lips, and a straining ear.' This is inevitably free. A closer rendering, that makes the construction easier to follow, would be (beginning with **cui**) : ' to whom, as many as there are feathers on her body, (there are) so many watchful eyes underneath, marvellous to relate, so many tongues, just so many mouths sound, so many ears she cocks.'

l. 181. **monstrum** is acc., in apposition to **illam**, l. **178.**

corpore, abl. of place where without preposition, like **pectore**, l. 4. This poetic abl. should by now be familiar, and will not always be noted.

l. 182. **dictu**, translated by the English infinitive, is really an abl. of a verbal noun from **dico**, and is an abl. of respect, meaning literally, ' in the telling '. The form is generally known as the supine in -u.

l. 183. **ora.** The pl. of the word **os**, ' mouth ', may often be translated ' lips '.

l. 184. **nocte**, abl. of time when : ' at night '.

medio, ' in the middle of ', i.e. ' between ', governing **caeli** and **terrae**. The neuter of the adjective **medius**, ' mid ', is here used as a noun =' middle '.

l. 185. **lumen**, literally ' light ', is very commonly used for ' eye ' in poetry.

l. 186. **luce**, same abl. as **nocte**, l. 183, ' in the daylight '.

custos, ' (like) a sentinel '. Cf. note on **pronuba**, l. 166.

l. 188. ' Clinging as much (**tam**) to the false and the vicious as declaring (**nuntia**, *lit.*, ' a reporter of ') the true.' The sense is that Rumour does not discriminate between true and false news. **ficti, pravi, veri** are all neuters of the adjective used as nouns—cf. the use of **medium**, l. 184—and all are objective genitives. This kind of genitive depends on a noun

or adjective, and stands in a relationship to that noun or
adjective similar to that between an object and a finite verb.
It will be clear that in **nuntia veri** the relationship between
the words is like that in **verum nuntiat**, ' she reports the truth '.
Cf. note, l. 178.

l. 189. **haec**, ' she ', i.e. Rumour. **tum**, ' on this occasion '.
replebat. The imperfect tense often expresses attempted or
commenced action ; here the latter, ' began to fill '.

l. 190. **facta atque infecta**, *lit.*, ' things done and not done ',
i.e. ' true and false '.

l. 191. **venisse Aenean**, acc. and infin., reporting indirectly
what Rumour said, ' that Aeneas had come '. **Aenean**,
acc. sg., according to the Greek 1st declension.

l. 192. **viro**, in apposition to **cui**, ' (as) husband '. Cf. note
on **pronuba**, l. 166 ; but translate ' in marriage '.

dignetur. All subordinate clauses dependent on indirect
statements, commands, and questions have their verbs in the
subjunctive. Thus **quis est hic, qui appropinquat?** becomes,
reported, **rogavit quis esset ille, qui appropinquaret**.

ll. 193, 194. Still acc. and infin. construction. The infinitive
is **fovere** and the acc. **eos** (understood), standing for Aeneas
and Dido.

l. 193. ' that they are now beguiling the long winter in
mutual (**inter se**) enjoyment '. **fovere** is, *lit.*, ' to warm '.
quam longa, *lit.*, ' how long it (= the winter) is '.

l. 194. **cupidine**, i.e. their love for one another. **captos**,
' held captive '.

l. 195. **haec**, accusative, ' these things ', i.e. ' these tidings '.

virum, gen. pl., common in the case of certain words, e.g
deus, divus, for the more usual form in -orum.

dea. Rumour, of course.

l. 196. **cursus**, acc. pl., and pl. for sg. **Iarban**, mentioned
before, l. 36, as a rejected suitor of Dido's. For the form of
the acc. see note on **Aenean**, l. 191.

l. 198. **hic**, ' he '. **Hammone**, ' from Hammon ', abl. of

origin. **Hammon,** written more commonly Ammon, was the
African name of the king of the gods, Jupiter.

rapta Garamantide nympha, ' a Garamantian nymph having
been carried off ', abl. abs.   Say, ' his mother a Garamantian
nymph '.   The Garamantes were an African tribe.

l. 200. **vigilem,** ' sleepless ', ' never dying '.

l. 201. **divum,** gen. pl.

l. 202. **solum, limina.**   These accs. have no precise construction, apart from a very loose and unjustifiable apposition
to **ignem.**   It is best in translation to make them the objects
of a verb, ' had made '.   **pingue** and **florentia** are then *proleptic*
adjectives, i.e. to be translated *after* the nouns they qualify,
as expressing the result of the action of the verb.   Cf. ' drain
the cup dry '.

limina, ' portals ', an example, and a most common one, of
synecdoche, since **limen** =, properly, ' threshold '.   For synecdoche see note on l. 46.

l. 203. **is,** i.e. Iarbas.   **animi,** locative, ' in mind '.

l. 204. **media inter numina,** ' in the very presence ' translates
this phrase as nearly as we can get it.

l. 205. **multa Iovem.**   Both accusatives limit **orasse. Iovem**
is direct object, **multa** adverbial acc.   Translate, ' to have
uttered many prayers to Jove '.

manibus supinis, ' with upturned palms ', the characteristic
attitude of ancient prayer.

supplex, adj. for adv.

orasse, for oravisse.   See note on **ulularunt,** l. 168.

l. 206. **Maurusia,** strictly ' Mauretanian ', ' Moorish ', but
used here for ' Libyan '.

l. 207. **epulata.**   Perfect participles of deponent verbs are
often used in a present meaning.   Cf. **veritam,** l. 96.

toris.   Cf. **pectore** and note, l. 4.

Lenaeum, ' Bacchic ', i.e. in the form of wine.

l. 208. **an** sometimes introduces a single question.

genitor. i.e. Ammon.

ll. **209, 210. caecique**, etc., *lit.*, ' and do *blind* fires amid the clouds terrify our hearts, and mingle *empty* rumblings '. But all the emphasis is on the words **caeci** and **inania**—notice their position. We can only get the same effect in some such way as this : ' and are those lightnings aimless (**caeci**), that in the clouds appal our hearts, and are their confused rumblings without meaning (**inania**).' Notice how, as once before, l. 160, Vergil suggests the notion of *confusion* by the use of the verb **misceo.**

l. **211. femina**, i.e. Dido.

l. **212. pretio posuit**, ' set up at a price ', i.e. Dido paid for the right to build her new city on Iarbas' land. The phrase is best rendered ' bought leave to build ' (Conington's translation).

arandum, gerundive in agreement with **litus,** ' to be ploughed'. English prefers the active, ' to plough '.

l. **213. loci leges dedimus**, *lit.*, ' we gave conditions of the place '. Iarbas means that his grant of a site was made subject to certain conditions. Translate ' we gave the place upon conditions '.

conubia nostra, ' our marriage ', i.e. ' my offer of marriage .'

l. **215. ille Paris.** Iarbas calls Aeneas ' that Paris ', because Paris was the type both of a handsome dandy and of a seducer of women. Iarbas, in his jealousy, loses sight of the fact that Paris abducted Helen, wife of Menelaus, and that he himself has no such tie with Dido.

semiviro. The Romans looked down on Oriental races as ' effeminate '.

l. **216. mitra.** This ' ribbon ', passing over the hair and fastened at the nape of the neck or, as here, under the chin, was a distinctly Phrygian article of dress.

madentem, ' wet ', i.e. with perfume. Translate ' scented '.

l. **217. subnixus,** ' supporting '. See note on **veritam,** l. 96.

rapto, abl. sg. neut. of the perfect participle, used as a noun : ' booty '. **rapto** is governed by **potitur.**

l. 218. quippe serves to underline **tuis** and is sarcastic : ' to *thy* temples '.

famam inanem. The ' idle tale ', of course, is that of Jove's justice and omnipotence.

l. 219. orantem and **tenentem** agree with **eum** (=**Iarbam**) understood.

l. 220. Omnipotens, ' the almighty one ', i.e. Jupiter or Ammon, subject to **audiit.**

moenia, of Carthage.

l. 221. amantes is governed by **ad** in l. 220.

l. 222. Mercurium. Mercury was the messenger of the gods.

talia mandat, ' instructs such things ', i.e. ' gives such instructions (as these) '.

l. 223. age. The imperative of **ago** is often used to strengthen another imperative, much as we use ' come ' in English.

Zephyros. Jupiter specifies the South-West wind as the one needed to carry the ships of Aeneas to Italy.

labere ; parse carefully. **Adloquere,** l. 226, is the same part.

pennis. Mercury had winged sandals.

l. 224. Dardanium ducem is object of **adloquere,** l. 226.

l. 225. exspectat is used intransitively, i.e. without an object.

urbes, pl. for sg. ' The city ' meant is the future Rome. Aeneas had been commanded by the gods to set up a new kingdom in Italy.

l. 227. fore must be supplied. ' Not such a one (**talem**) did his most fair mother promise us he would be.'

genetrix, Venus.

l. 228. Graium, gen. pl., depending on **armis.** The latter is an abl. of separation : ' from the arms '.

vindicat would be a perfect in English. The object is **illum** of l. 227. The rescues spoken of occurred during the Trojan War.

l. 229. Sed fore qui, ' but that (he) would be (the man

to . . .' The acc. and infin. depends on **promisit** understood from l. 228. Translate the three subjunctives **regeret, proderet, mitteret,** by English infinitives. More literally **qui regeret** is ' such as would rule ', and the subjunctive is generic, (a variety of the consecutive), employed in relative clauses with an indefinite antecedent. (There is of course an additional reason here why the three verbs would be in the subjunctive, for each is the verb of a subordinate clause in indirect speech.) For a simple example of the generic subjunctive cf. **non is sum qui talia dicam,** ' I am not the-sort-of-man (is) to say such things '.

Notice Vergil's pride in the achievements of Rome, revealed in ll. 229–231.

imperiis, pl. for sg.

l. 230. Teucer was a king of Troy.

ll. 232–234. If Aeneas has no ambition for himself, will he not win Italy for his son?

l. 232. **nulla,** adjective qualifying **gloria,** is best translated ' not '.

accendit. The object is **eum** (=Aeneas) understood.

rerum, ' destiny '.

l. 233. **ipse** is used to emphasize **sua.** It need not be translated.

l. 234. **pater invidet,** ' does he, a father, begrudge . . .' Better rendered : ' does he begrudge his own son, Ascanius . . .'

l. 235. **gente** refers to the Carthaginian people, though to call them hostile is to anticipate history.

l. 236. **prolem** refers to the Roman race of which Aeneas is to be the founder. **Ausonius** is common in poetry for ' Italian ', and **Lavinius** stands for ' Latin ', Lavinium being a town of Latium.

l. 237. **naviget,** ' let him sail ', jussive subjunctive . Cf. note on **liceat,** l. 103.

summa, ' the sum ', i.e. what all the long speech adds up to.

nostri for the more obvious, and therefore to Vergil un-

attractive, noster : ' this be my message '. **esto** is 3rd sg. imperative of sum.

l. 238. **Dixerat,** ' he had spoken ', **i.e.** ' he ceased '.

ille, Mercury.

l. 240. **sublimem** agrees with **eum,** understood.

supra governs both **aequora** and **terram,** l. 241.

l. 241. **pariter cum,** ' together with ', i.e. ' as swiftly as '.

l. 242. **virgam.** This ' wand ', with which Mercury is always depicted, was also called caduceus.

Orco, ' from Orcus '. Orcus is a word for Hades.

l. 243. **sub,** ' down to '.

Tartara, another name for Hades.

l. 244. **somnos,** pl. for sg.

morte, ' at death ', i.e. that the souls of the dead might see during their passage, under Mercury's escort, to the nether world.

l. 245. **illâ fretus,** ' relying on it ', i.e. the wand. Say, ' with its aid '.

l. 246. **volans,** *lit.,* ' flying '. Render by a clause, ' as he flies '.

l. 247. **Atlas,** the mythical giant who bore up the sky. He is identified with the Atlas range in N.W. Africa.

l. 248. **cui,** a dative where a possessive genitive (**cuius**) would be expected. This is a common idiom. Proceed as if **cuius** were the reading.

l. 249. The first **et** =' both ' and is superfluous in English.

l. 250. **infusa,** *lit.,* ' poured on ', i.e. ' fallen '.

l. 252. **nitens,** *lit.,* ' leaning ' ; translate ' poised '.

Cyllenius, a name of Mercury, from his birthplace, Mt. Cyllene in Arcadia, (Greece).

l. 253. **toto praeceps corpore,** *lit.,* ' headlong with all his body '. Take the words with **se misit :** ' he flung his whole weight downwards '.

l. 255. **iuxta** governs **aequora.**

l. 256. **haud aliter,** ' not otherwise ', **i.e.** ' **even so** '; often used by Vergil after a simile.

l. 258. **materno ab avo.** Mercury's ' maternal grandfather ' **is** Atlas, whose daughter, Maia, **was Mercury's** mother.

Cyllenia proles (nominative) =Mercury.

l. 259. **ut** +indic. =' as ', or, as here, ' when '.

magalia. A Carthaginian word. The humble dwellings of Carthage are meant.

plantis, ' feet '. As **planta is** properly ' sole ', this is an example of synecdoche, explained in the note on l. 46.

l. 261. **illi.** Translate as if **illius,** and cf. **mihi,** l. 15 and note.

l. 262. **laena,** nominative.

l. 263. **quae munera,** inverted, and pl. for sg., ' **a** present which '.

l. 264. **et tenui,** etc., ' **and had shot the web with golden** thread ' (*lit.,* ' thin gold '). Dido had relieved the purple of the cloak with occasional stripes of gold. The point of ll. 261–264 is to show how far Aeneas has already fallen victim to the oriental luxury of Carthage.

l. 265. **invadit,** the subject is Mercury.

l. 267. **oblite,** voc. sg. masc. of perf. **partic.** of **obliviscor,** ' forgetful '.

rerum, ' destiny '.

l. 268. **deum,** gen. pl.

Olympo, ' from O.' Olympus, **a** mountain **in northern** Greece, was the legendary home of the gods.

l. 271. **otia, terris,** pl. for sg.

ll. 272, 273. Cf. ll. 232, 233, **and notes on these lines.**

l. 274, **spes,** acc. pl.

l. 276. **tali ore,** ' with such mouth ', no more than ' **thus** '.

l. 277. mortales, ' mortal ' =' of men '.

medio sermone, ' in mid speech ', i.e. ' while yet speaking,' which was not, of course, the case.   Say ' upon the instant '.

l. 279. **aspectu** with amens.

l. 280. **arrectae,** supply sunt.

faucibus, abl. of place where without prep.

l. 281. **ardet abire,** ' he is on fire to depart '.   **The infinitive** after ardeo is not a prose construction.

fugā, abl. ' in flight '.

l. 282. **tanto,** ' so stern '.

l. 283. **quid agat,** ' what **is** he to do? '   This **is the** ' deliberative ' subjunctive, expressing doubt or hesitation as to a course of action.   audeat and sumat in l. 284 **are** similar uses.

quo adfatu, ' with what words ', *lit.,* ' address '.

ambire, almost exactly like the colloquial English ' get round '.   Translate ' placate '.

l. 284. **quae prima exordia sumat,** ' what first beginnings is he to choose ', i.e. ' what words shall he select wherewith to open '.

ll. 285, 286.   These lines finely express Aeneas's consideration of every possibility.   Tennyson's line, ' This way and that dividing the swift mind ' is a paraphrase of 285.

l. 286. ' and hurries it in divers directions, and turns it every way.'

l. 287. **alternanti** agrees with **ei,** understood :   ' to him hesitating '.

l. 288.   The names are those of some of his Trojan comrades.

aptent, cogant, parent, dissimulent, are subjunctives of indirect command, dependent on **imperat eis ut** understood, easily enough, from **vocat.**   Begin ' he bids them ' and translate all four verbs by infinitives, **the normal way of** expressing indirect command in English.

l. 289. **taciti,** adj. for adv.

l. 290. **sit,** subjunctive in indirect **question dependent on**

dissimulent, which should be translated before **quae . . . novandis.**

rebus novandis, ' for matters being changed ', i.e. ' for the change of plan '.

l. 291. **quando,** ' since ' .

l. 292. **rumpi speret.** rumpi = rumpi posse, and spero here = ' expect ', not ' hope '.

amores, the love between herself and Aeneas.

l. 293. **temptaturum,** sc. esse.

aditus, acc. pl. sese (l. 291) **temptaturum aditus** =' he himself will try access ', i.e. ' will essay to approach her '.

ll. 293, 294. The indirect questions **quae . . . (sint) tempora** and **quis . . . (sit) . . . modus** are both also dependent on **temptaturum** : ' and will try what is the most propitious moment for speech, and what the favourable method for his aims '. ' for speech ' is **fandi,** lit., ' of speaking ', gen. of the gerund of the deponent verb **for.**

l. 295. **laeti,** adj. for adv.

parent. Cf. this form, having a long first syllable, with părent, l. 290.

l. 296. **possit,** ' could ', potential subjunctive. Cf. **abnuat, malit,** l. 108.

l. 297. **prima,** ' first ', i.e. ' instantly '.

l. 298. **omnia tuta timens,** lit., ' fearing all things safe', Vergilian for ' fearful where all seemed safe '.

eadem Fama, lit., ' the same Rumour ' =' Rumour also '.

furenti, with ei, fem., understood.

l. 299. **detulit.** defero is the regular word for ' inform ', and delator, its derivative =' informer '.

l. 300. **saevit.** The subject is Dido.

animi, locative. Cf. l. 203.

l. 301. **bacchatur.** The verb suggests the intoxication, compounded of wine-draughts and religious ecstasy, experienced by the worshippers of Bacchus, the god of wine.

ll. 301, 302. qualis excita Thyias, 'like a Bacchanal, roused . . .' The full construction would be **(talis erat) qualis (est) Thyias,** 'such she (i.e. Dido) was as a Bacchanal is'. **Thyiās,** two syllables.

l. 301. commotis sacris, 'by the sacred emblems **waved**', i.e. 'by the waving of the sacred emblems'. Notice how **the** noun 'waving' is represented in Latin by the participle **commotis,** and compare **Caesar interfectus urbem perturbavit,** 'the murder of Caesar appalled the city'. **Sacris.** These 'emblems' would include statues of the god and other objects used in his worship, which would sway above the procession of half-demented votaries.

l. 302. audito Baccho, '(the name) Bacchus having **been** heard,' abl. abs., i.e. 'having heard the cry "Bacchus".'

ll. 302, 303. stimulant, vocat : the object of these verbs is **eam** understood.

l. 303. nocturnus with **Cithaeron,** 'C., under its darkness'.

clamore, the cries of the worshippers.

Cithaeron, mountain near Thebes, in central Greece, famous for the wild scenes that attended the triennial festival of Bacchus.

l. 304. ultro. No single word in English quite corresponds to this Latin word. It suggests that the statement it accompanies is an unexpected one. Here, for instance, Dido 'first addresses' Aeneas, though the latter, l. 293, is planning to approach her.

l. 305. sperasti = speravisti, syncopated form.

l. 306. posse = te posse, acc. and infin. after **sperasti.**

tacitus, adj. for adv.

mea terra, abl. of place whence.

l. 307. amor, dextera, Dido, are all subjects of **tenet,** ' detain '.

dextera, ' right hand ' = ' handclasp ' and may be translated ' pledge '.

l. 308. moritura, ' doomed to perish '. Dido means **she** will put an end to her own life if Aeneas deserts her.

l. 309. **hiberno sidere,** *lit.*, ' with a winter **star** ', **i.e.** ' **under** a wintry sky '.

l. 310. **mediis Aquilonibus,** ' in the midst of the north **winds** ', i.e. ' when the north wind blows strongest '. A north **wind** would be most unfavourable to a voyage from Africa **to** Italy.

l. 311. **crudelis, voc.,** ' cruel one '.

non. Take this closely with **aliena** and **ignotus.**

ll. 311–313. The sense is : even if you were going home, instead of to strange lands, would you start now, in winter?

For the imperfect subjunctive in conditional sentences, **see** note on ll. 15–19.

l. 313. **Troia peteretur,** ' would Troy be sought ', i.e. ' **would** you seek Troy '—the passive construction **is** awkward.

per, ' over '.   **classibus,** pl. for sg.

l. 314. **mene** = me (acc.) + **ne,** interrogative enclitic.

per, and in l. 316, ' by '.

te is acc., the object of some such verb **as oro,** ' I beg ', understood.

dextram, same meaning as in l. 307.

l. 315. Having given him all, she has nothing left to **bind** him to her except appeals to his pity and sense of honour.

mihi miserae, ' to me hapless ', i.e., ' my hapless self '.

l. 316. **inceptos,** ' begun ', i.e. ' that we have entered upon '.

l. 317. **si bene quid de te merui,** ' if I have in aught (**quid,** adverbial acc.) deserved well of **you.** '

quidquam meum, ' anything (of) **mine** '.

l. 318. **miserere,** parse carefully.

istam, (in agreement with **mentem, l. 319),** ' **this (of yours)** ', as usual.

l. 319. **locus,** ' room ', subject to **est** understood, and qualified by the pronoun, **quis,** ' any ', instead of **the more** strictly correct **qui.**

mentem, ' **purpose** '.

l. 320. te is governed by propter, as also in l. 321.

l. 321. odere. The object is me, understood. Remember that odi is a defective verb, and its perfect tense has a present meaning.

infensi, sc. sunt.

eundem agrees with te, ' on account of the same you ', idiomatic Latin for, ' on your account, too '.

l. 322. exstinctus, sc. est. There are two subjects to this verb, pudor, and fama prior, l. 323.

qua sola, both abl., ' by which alone '. fama, l. 323, is the antecedent of qua, and must be translated before it.

adibam, ' conative ' use of imperf. (l. 189), ' I sought to reach '. ' Reaching the stars ' means achieving immortality.

l. 323. cui, ' for whom ', i.e. which of her scorned and vengeful suitors among the natives or the Tyrian settlers will now make her his own?

moribundam. The adjectives in -bundus are almost equal to present participles.

l. 324. The quoniam clause explains her choice of the word hospes. de coniuge, ' from husband ', i.e. ' now that I may no more call you husband '.

l. 325. an dum, ' or (am I waiting) till '.

l. 326. destruat, ducat, final subjunctives, though they occur in a temporal clause, because a notion of purpose is present in addition to that of time.

ll. 327, 328. si ... suboles, lit., ' if any child had been conceived by me from you '. Turn this into the active, ' if I had conceived a (qua) child by you '. mihi is dat. of the agent, ' by me '. This dative is not uncommon in poetry, with the passive voice.

l. 328. quis, ' some ', indefinite. mihi is dative of the person interested, and being a Latin idiom, cannot be translated literally. Say, ' and if I had some little Aeneas playing '. The literal rendering is, ' and if for me some little Aeneas were playing '.

l. 329. **luderet,** and **viderer,** l. 330. For the meaning of the tenses see note on conditional subjunctives, ll. 15-19.

qui referret, ' to recall '. referret is final (purpose) subjunctive. Final clauses introduced by relatives are very common.

tamen. Ignore in translation. It modifies a suppressed clause, ' even if you went '.

l. 330. **capta,** ' deceived '.

l. 331. **Dixerat.** See note, l. 238.

monitis, abl., ' at the bidding '.

immota tenebat lumina. He did not, that is, lower his eyes in shame.

l. 332. **obnixus,** *lit.,* ' struggling (against) ', i.e. ' with a great effort '.

sub, ' deep in '.

l. 333. **pauca,** ' a few (things) '. Remember that adjectives are very often used in Latin without nouns, and that their meaning is then indicated by their gender, e.g. **boni,** nom. pl. masc. = ' good *men* ', etc. In the present case the word **pauca** would be more naturally translated into English by the adverb, ' briefly '.

ll. 333-335. The order is a little involved ; in translating it should be : **numquam, regina, ego negabo te promeritam (esse) quae plurima** (' the utmost which ') **vales enumerare fando.** The general sense is, ' I will never deny my great debt to you.'

l. 335. **me** is governed by **pigebit,** *lit.,* ' it will never disgust me ' = ' I shall never shrink from '.

Elissae. Elissa was another name for Dido.

l. 336. **memor,** sc. **sum. mei,** genitive sing. The genitive is objective—see note, l. 188—dependent on **memor.**

dum . . . artus, i.e. while I live.

l. 337. **pro re,** *lit.,* ' according to the circumstance ', i.e. ' as the occasion demands '.

pauca, to be translated as in 333.

abscondere, notice the infinitive after **speravi,** and cf. l. 305. The normal construction with spero is acc. and (usually future) infin.

l. 338. **ne finge,** for the prose noli fingere or ne finxeris. **Ne** with imperative is common in Vergil for prohibitions.

l. 339. **taedas,** ' the torches ' were an accompaniment, and hence a symbol, of marriage, and this is meant here.

haec, ' such an '. **foedera,** pl. for sg. **veni,** ' entered '.

ll. 340–344. For the conditional subjunctives see note on ll. 15–19.

l. 341. **meis auspiciis,**[1] ' under my own auspices ', i.e. ' as a free agent '. The auspices, or omens for the outcome of projected acts, were ' taken ' by Roman magistrates charged with the responsibility for such acts. Thus ' to lead one's life under one's own auspices ' means to be in control of it, to live it as one would wish.

componere curas, ' to order my cares ' is ' to cope with my troubles '.

l. 342. **primum,** ' first ' = ' for choice '.

meorum, masc. ' of my people '.

l. 343. **colerem,** ' I would tend ' = ' devote myself to '.

l. 344. **manu,** understand **mea.**

victis, dat.

Pergama, neut. pl., was the name for the citadel of Troy.

l. 345. **nunc,** ' as it is ', a not uncommon meaning of the word.

Gryneus Apollo. The god is here so called because he had a temple at Grynium in Asia Minor. Similarly his oracles— Apollo, remember, was the god of prophecy—are in the next line called Lycian, because he had a famous shrine at Patara in Lycia.

[1] Auspicium is derived from **avis** and spicio and means ' watching (the flight of) birds ', whose behaviour the Roman seers watched in the belief that it foreshadowed future events.

l. 346. iussere =iusserunt.

l. 347. hic and haec, ' this ', both refer to Italy, but the first is attracted into the gender of the complement amor.

arces, equally with aspectus, is subject to detinet, but the verb agrees, as often in Latin, only with the nearer subject.

l. 348. Phoenissam is in apposition with te.

ll. 349–350. *Lit.*, ' What envy, pray (tandem), is there that the Trojans should settle ', etc. *I.e.* ' why do you grudge . . .'.

l. 349. Ausonia terra, see note on pectore, l. 4.

l. 350. et nos fas quaerere, ' it is lawful that we, too, should seek '.

l. 351. patris Anchisae depends on imago, l. 353.

l. 353. et joins admonet and terret.

l. 354. me puer Ascanius, supply admonet from l. 353.

iniuria is also subject to this admonet.

capitis iniuria cari, *lit.* ' the wrong of that dear head ', i.e. ' the wrong done to that dear head '. What that wrong is he makes clear in the next line. Capitis is objective genitive, see note l. 188. Caput is used poetically here for ' person ', ' creature '.

l. 355. The construction of fraudo is a direct obj. (quem) of the person cheated, and an abl. (regno, arvis) of the thing of which he is cheated. We should say, ' whom I am cheating *of* . . .'.

l. 356. interpres divum is, of course, Mercury. divum is gen. pl.

l. 357. utrumque caput, ' each head (of two) ', i.e. ' both our heads ', ' your head and mine ', He means he swears to the truth of his statement by their two lives, the dearest things they possess.

l. 360. meque teque, ' both me and thee '.

l. 361. sponte, sc. mea.

l. 362. dicentem agrees with eum understood, which is the object of tuetur.

tuetur. The subject is ' she ' (Dido), with which **aversa,**
lit., ' turned away ', agrees.

iamdudum. When this word accompanies a present or
imperfect, the meaning is that of English perfect and pluperfect
respectively, with the addition of the adverb ' long '. Thus,
l. 362 = ' As he speaks such (words), she has long been regarding
him askance (aversa) '.

l. 363. totum, with **hominem** understood.

l. 364. luminibus, ' looks '. In English we should prefer
to make ' looks ', rather than ' she ', the subject : ' and her
silent glances wander over the whole man '.

accensa, *lit.*, ' on fire ', i.e. ' in anger '.

l. 365. erat has to be supplied twice, **with two** subjects,
parens and **Dardanus. Tibi** roughly = **tua** (with parens).
Cf. note on **mihi,** l. 15.

ll. 366, 367. You are no child, she says, of god or man, but
of craggy rock, and reared by wild beasts.

l. 367. Hyrcanae. Hyrcania was a country near the
Caucasus, and the reputed haunt of tigers.

admorunt = admoverunt. Cf. note, l. 168. admorunt ubera,
' moved their udders towards (you) ' = ' gave you suck '.

l. 368. dissimulo, supply an object, ' it '. quid = ' why '.

aut quae, etc., ' or for what greater things do I hold myself
back '.   She means, ' what worse treatment can I expect,
that I should keep silence now ? '

ll. 369, 370. Dido begins to talk **' at '** rather than **' to '**
Aeneas, as the change to the 3rd person shows. **Num,** as usual
in direct questions, suggests that the only possible answer is
' No '.

l. 370. victus dedit, ' did he, vanquished, give ', i.e. ' break
down and shed '.

l. 371. quae quibus anteferam ?   *Lit.*, ' what things am I to
put before what things ? ', i.e. ' what should I speak of first ? '
Which of her many grievances, she means, shall she first
ventilate.

l. 371. anteferam is deliberative subjunctive; cf. note on **agat.**

l. 372. oculis aequis, ' with impartial eyes '. Dido means that the very gods are partial to Aeneas in not punishing him for his perfidy.

Saturnius pater = Jove, Saturn's son.

l. 373. nusquam, etc. Supply est.

eiectum and **egentem** agree with **eum** understood, which is the object of **excepi** and **locavi.**

litore. Cf. note on **pectore,** l. 4. **eiectum litore,** ' cast up on the shore ', i.e. ' shipwrecked '.

l. 374. demens, adj. for adv.

regni . . . locavi, etc., ' set him in part of my kingdom ' can only mean ' gave him a share in my kingdom '.

l. 376. heu furiis incensa feror, *lit.,* ' alas, I am being carried off, set on fire by madness '. Say, ' alas, madness consumes and carries me away '.

ll. 376–378. Dido scornfully refers to Aeneas's divine warnings. **Apollo** and **sortes** are nominatives without a verb. Say ' now it is prophetic Apollo, now the Lycian oracles '— which Aeneas pleads as excuse for his desertion. For **Lyciae** see l. 346 and note.

l. 377. et = ' too '.

l. 378. interpres divum, cf. l. 356 and note.

l. 379. scilicet is very often used to introduce an ironical remark. Thus, though Dido *says* ' That, to be sure, (scilicet) is a trouble to the gods, that anxiety disturbs their repose (*lit.* [them] quiet),' she *means* that the gods care naught for Aeneas and his plans.

l. 380. teneo and **refello** are *conative* presents (i.e. denoting *attempted* action) : ' seek to detain ', etc.

l. 381. i. From **eo, ire.**

sequĕre—parse this carefully.

l. 382. spero has two acc. and infins. dependent on it : **(te) hausurum** and **(te) vocaturum.**

si quid pia numina possunt, ' if the righteous gods can (do) anything ', i.e. ' have any power '.

l. 383. **(te) supplicia hausurum,** ' that you will swallow the bitter draught of punishment ', *lit.,* ' will drain punishment ', a bold metaphor.

scopulis. She hopes for his destruction by shipwreck.

Dido, accusative, according to the Greek form.

ll. 384-386. She will pursue him while she lives, and when she dies, no less.

l. 384. **sequar.** Supply **te** as object.

atris, ' smoky '; **absens,** ' (though) far away '. Dido means that her ill will will attend Aeneas however far he goes from her. Probably by her reference to ' smoky flames ', which were associated with the Furies, or goddesses of vengeance, Dido means to suggest that her hatred will be comparable in power to theirs.

l. 385. **seduxerit** is fut. perf. The English preference is for the perf.

l. 386. **umbra,** ' (as) a shade '. For the use of apposition, when English inserts ' as ', cf. **pronuba** and note, l. 166.

l. 387. **audiam,** ' I shall hear ', i.e. of his paying the penalty.

haec fama, ' this report ', the regular Latin way of saying ' tidings of this '.

manes sub imos, ' down to the lowest pit of Hades '. **manes** properly =' spirits of the dead '.

l. 388. **medium,** with **sermonem** in grammar, but equivalent to an adverbial phrase, ' in the middle '. The suggestion is that Dido seemed about to say more, when she was overcome by the strength of her emotions.

l. 389. **aegra,** ' sick (at heart) '. **ex oculis,** ' from the sight of men '.

l. 390. The first **multa** is adverbial accusative, ' much ', the second is direct object of **dicere,** l. 391.

cunctantem and **parantem** agree with **eum** understood, which is the object of **linquens.**

l. 390. metu is abl. of cause, ' in fear '. Cf. **mobilitate** and note, l. 175.

l. 391. suscipiunt, supply **eam** as object.

conlapsa, ' fainting '.

l. 392. thalamo, dative instead of the **ad + acc. of** prose. **stratis** may be the same, or abl. of place where without preposition.

l. 393. dolentem, ' (her) grieving '. We should say ' her grief '.

l. 394. solando, abl. of gerund of **solor,** ' by consoling ', i.e. ' with consolation '.

l. 395. multa. See note on the first **multa** of l. 390.

animum, ' in his heart ', or ' to the heart ', acc. of respect or part concerned. The stock example of this poetic use of the case is **tremit artus,** ' he trembles *as to* his limbs '.

ll. 397, 398. litore toto, ' all along the shore '. Even in prose ' place ' phrases including **totus** have no preposition.

l. 398. uncta, ' well caulked '. **carina,** *lit.* ' keel ', = ' hull ' here. This is synecdoche, cf. l. 46. **carina** is sg. for pl., less common than the reverse.

l. 399. frondentes remos, *lit.,* ' leafy oars '. The meaning is that they bring from the woods (**silvis**) boughs still bearing leaves which they propose to fashion into oars. Translate ' leafy boughs for oars '.

l. 400. fugae studio, ' in their eagerness for flight '. **studio** is abl. of cause, and **fugae** objective gen.

l. 401. cernas, ' you could see (them) '—if you were present. ' Potential ' subjunctive, i.e. conditional, but with the ' if ' clause (protasis) not expressed,

tota ex urbe, ' from every quarter of the city '.

ll. 402-407. A simile. The activity of the Trojans is compared to that of ants. Begin with **ac velut cum.**

l. 403. hiemis, objective genitive.

tecto. Constructed as stratis, l. **392.**

l. 404. **nigrum,** because consisting of ants.

campis, ' over the plain ', ' along the ground '.

l. 405. **calle angusto,** abl. of route. Cf. note on **portis,** l. 130.

pars trudunt. pars is often used with a plural verb in the meaning ' some '.

l. 406. **frumenta,** ' grains of corn '.

l. 407. **moras,** *lit.,* ' delays '. We should say ' laggards ', 'stragglers '.

l. 408. **fuit** must be supplied for the nominative **quis sensus,** ' what feeling was there then to you, Dido . . .', i.e. ' what was your emotion '.

l. 409. **fervĕre.** Usually the verb is second conjugation ; this is an old form.

l. 410. **prospiceres, videres. Cum,** meaning ' when ', takes subjunctive in historic tenses.

arce ex summa =, as usual, ' from the roof of the citadel ', not ' from the highest citadel '. Remember that the superlative adjectives **summus, medius, imus, extremus** answer commonly to the English nouns, ' top ', ' middle ', ' bottom ', ' edge '.

l. 411. **misceri,** ' astir '. Vergil is very fond of using this word to describe busy and confused scenes.

l. 412. Translate **quid,** ' to what ', though the simplest way of explaining its construction is to take it as direct object of **facere** understood.

l. 413. **ire in lacrimas is an unusual phrase, but** understandable.

temptare. Supply **eum** as object.

precando, ' with entreaty '. Cf. note on **solando,** l. 394.

l. 414. **supplex,** adj. for adv., ' humbly '.

animos, ' spirit ', i.e. the pride and anger she had shown in ll. 362–387.

l. 415. ' Lest, vainly resolved on death **(moritura),** she should leave aught untried '. Dido has resolved to destroy herself if Aeneas goes, but determines upon a last appeal first. **Quid** is the neuter of **quis**, indefinite pronoun, the usual word for ' anyone ', ' anything ', after si, nisi, num, ne.

l. 416. **vides . . . litore,** ' you see that they are making haste, all along the shore '.

properari literally is ' that it is being hastened '. It is indirect speech for **properatur** and the construction is the impersonal passive, mentioned on l. 151. For **toto litore**—ı preposition—see note, l. 398.

l. 417. **convenere** = **convenerunt.** So **imposuere,** next line:

vocat, etc., i.e. the sails are already being shaken out.

l. 418. This garlanding of the sterns seems to have been the ancient equivalent of the Blue Peter, the flag flown by ships to indicate that they are about to sail.

l. 419. **hunc tantum,** ' so great as this '—the usual meaning of these words in combination.

sperare, ' foresee ', obviously not ' hope for '.

l. 420. **et,** ' also '.

ll. 420, 421. **miserae mihi,** ' for wretched me ', i.e. ' for me in my misery '.

l. 421. **exsequere ;** for the form, cf. **sequere,** l. 381, and remember that the 2nd sg. imperative of deponents and passives is identical with the pres. infin. active of the corresponding conjugation.

l. 422. **colere** and **credere** are *historic* infinitives, i.e. infinitives having much the same force as imperfect indicatives, expressing repeated or habitual action.

colo here = ' be attentive to '.

etiam goes closely with **arcanos.**

l. 423. ' You alone knew the man's easy approaches and times ', i.e. ' You alone knew the times when he was approach- ıble '. Cf. l. 293. **noras** = **noveras,** a syncopated form, explained ɔn l. 33. Remember that **novi, noveram** = ' I know ', ' I new '.

aditus et tempora is an example of hendiadys, i.e. two nouns put in the same case when one should more logically be in the genitive dependent on the other. Thus **adituum tempora** would be more readily intelligible here.

l. 424. **supplex**, adj. for adv., as in l. 414.

adfare. See note on **exsequere**, l. 421.

ll. 425–428 Dido declares she has done nothing to provoke the hostility of Aeneas.

l. 425. **exscindere**, poetic, pres. infin., instead of the **me exscissuram esse** required by prose.

Danai. These were a tribe of Greeks, but the word is frequently used in poetry for Greeks generally.

l. 426. **Aulide**, locative. It was from Aulis that the Greek fleet sailed for the war against Troy.

l. 427. **revelli**, ' did I tear up ' is used in a literal sense with **cinerem**, but in a decidedly strained one with **manes**. Translate the verb a second time by ' disturb '. Anchises, the father of Aeneas, had died in Sicily shortly before the Trojan hero arrived in Africa.

l. 429. **det**, jussive subjunctive. Cf. note on **liceat**, l. 103. **exspectet** is similar.

amanti—a noun. Dido means herself.

l. 430. **ferentes**, ' favourable '.

l. 431. **oro** has two constructions, (i) noun object, **coniugium**, and (ii) two noun clause objects, the indirect petitions **ut careat** and (ut) **relinquat.**

antiquum, ' former '.

l. 432. Latium was the Italian district around Rome.

l. 434. ' Till my fortune teaches my overwhelmed heart (*lit.*, me vanquished) to grieve.' She means that at present she is too crushed for the normal expression of grief.

dum, ' until ', takes the subjunctive when a notion of purpose exists, as here, beside the idea of time. Hence **doceat** is a final subjunctive.

l. 436. ' Which when you shall have given (it) to me, I will repay heaped up at my death ', i.e. ' and when you have given it me, I will repay it with interest at my death '.

l. 437. **talibus,** understand **dictis.**

talesque, etc., ' and such weepings did her most wretched sister report and report again ', i e. to Aeneas, to whom Anna goes with the story of Dido's distress. Say, ' and the tale of such tears her sister, most sorrowful, bears again and again '.

l. 439. **aut tractabilis audit,** ' nor (*the influence of* **nullis** *persisting*) does he, amenable, listen to . . .', i.e. ' and, inexorable, he listens not to '.

l. 440. **placidas** is probably *proleptic* use of the adjective (cf. note, l. 202), i.e. it expresses the result of the action of the verb, as in ' scrub the floor *clean* '. Hence translate ' and heaven (**deus**) stops the hero's ears and makes them obdurate '.

ll. 441–446. Another simile, in which Vergil compares the resistance of an oak buffeted by gales to the firmness of Aeneas' resolution. The simile begins with **ac velut cum.**

l. 441. **annoso validam robore,** ' strong with the timber of centuries '.

l. 442. **nunc hinc nunc illinc** are to be taken closely with **flatibus,** ' with gusts now from this quarter now from that '.

l. 443. **inter se,** ' among themselves ', i.e. ' with one another '.

it, ' there rises '.

stridor, either ' howling ' of the winds or ' groaning ' of the tree.

l. 444. **concusso stipite,** abl. abs., ' as the trunk is shaken '.

l. 445. **ipsa,** i.e. the tree.

ll. 445–446. **quantum,** etc. To follow this, translate the two clauses in reverse order : ' and with its roots it stretches towards Tartarus (i.e. Hades and therefore downwards) just so far as (it stretches) with its top towards the breezes of heaven.' The meaning is simply that its roots are as deep as its branches and leaves are high.

l. 447. haud secus, *lit.*, ' not otherwise ', i.e. ' even so '.

hinc atque hinc = hinc atque illinc of l. 442.

l. 449. lacrimae, Dido's, or possibly Anna's.

inanes, adj. for adv.

l. 451. taedet tueri, ' it wearies (her) to gaze upon . . .'.

convexa, *lit.*, ' curved '. Here the neuter plural of the adjective is used as a noun, ' vault '.

l. 452. quo magis inceptum peragat, ' that she may the more carry through her purpose ', i.e. ' to make her more resolved to carry out this purpose, and leave the light '.

In the succeeding lines (453-465), Vergil tells how Dido is confirmed in the resolve to destroy herself by supernatural portents.

l. 454. horrendum dictu, ' horrible to relate '. **dictu**, the supine in -u, is really the abl. sg. of a verbal noun, the other supine being its accusative. **dictu** is actually an abl. of respect, and the literal meaning is, ' in the telling '. Cf. note on l. 182.

l. 455. se vertere = ' turn ', intransitive. Verbs such as ' move ', ' roll ', ' turn ', ' change ', etc., which can be used both transitively and intransitively in English are represented in Latin by the active voice (transitive meaning) and by the passive, or, as here, active + reflexive pronoun object (intransitive meaning).

l. 456. hoc visum is object of **effata**, which is put for **effata est**, the auxiliary being often omitted.

l. 457. tectis, i.e. the palace.

de marmore = marmoreum.

ll. 457, 458. templum coniugis antiqui, ' a shrine (to the memory) of her former husband '.

l. 460. voces, ' tones '. **voces** and **verba** are both subjects of **visa** = visa sunt. But the passive—' the tones and words . . . seemed to be heard '—is awkward. Say, ' she seemed to hear '. **exaudiri** suggests the faintness of the sounds.

l. 461. **teneret,** ' held sway over '. For the subjunctive cf. note on **prospiceres,** l. 410. **Imponeret,** l. 453, is similar.

l. 463. **queri, ducere.** Historic infinitives. Cf. note on **colere,** l. 422.

et longas, etc., ' and lengthened its long cries to weeping ', i.e., uttered such long drawn out notes as resembled the sound of sobs.

l. 465. **horrificant,** sc. **eam.**

furentem agrees with **eam** understood.

l. 467. **sibi** goes with **videtur,** ' she seems to herself '.

l. 468. **deserta terra,** abl. of place where.

ll. 469–473. Vergil compares the terrifying images seen by Dido to those that persecuted Pentheus and Orestes. Pentheus, driven insane by Bacchus, is described by Euripides, who tells his story in one of the plays, as seeing two suns and two cities of Thebes, and to this Vergil is referring in l. 470. Orestes avenged upon his mother, Clytemnestra, her slaying of his father Agamemnon, and for his sin was the victim of persecution by the Furies, to whose company Vergil adds the murdered mother herself. The story of Orestes was a popular subject of Greek tragedy.

l. 469. **agmina.** ' Troops ' is a poetic licence. There were only three Eumenides or Furies, Tisiphone, Allecto and Megaera. The word Eumenides means ' kindly ones ' and was bestowed by the Greeks on the avenging trinity in an effort to propitiate them.

l. 470. **solem** and **Thebas** are subjects to the infinitive **ostendere,** in the acc. and infin. construction, depending on **videt.**

l. 471. Take **veluti** again before **cum** (l. 473) **Agamemnonius Orestes.**

scaenis agitatus, ' hounded across the stage '. This is, doubtless, a reminiscence of a play seen by the poet. **scaenis** is pl. for sg., and abl., probably of route.

l. 472. Torches and serpents were the insignia, as it were. of the Furies.

l. 474. **concepit furias**, *lit.*, ' conceived madness ', i.e. ' became insane '.

l. 476. **exigit**, ' works out ', ' plans '.

dictis adgressa, ' addressing ' will do for both words. For the use of the perf. partic. with present meaning cf. note on **veritam**, l. 96.

l. 477. **vultu**, ' by her expression ', which she composes to show no sign of the despair within.

spem fronte serenat. We should expect, and must translate this as **spe frontem serenat**, ' calms her brow with hope ', i.e. deliberately smoothes away the tense look of anxiety. The phrase as we have it results from Vergil's studious avoidance of the obvious, or possibly from metrical difficulties which he would have resolved, if he had ever undertaken the revision of the poem which his death prevented.

l. 479. **quae reddat**, ' to give back '. It is very common in Latin to introduce final clauses by **qui** instead of **ut**, in cases where, like the present, the main clause contains a suitable antecedent (**viam**). Cf. **cocum misi quo utaris**, ' I have sent a cook for you to make use of '.

vel eo, etc., ' or free me, loving, from him ', i.e. ' rid me of my passion for him '.

l. 480. **iuxta** governs **finem** and solem.

l. 481. **locus**, ' abode '.

l. 482. **umero**, ' upon his shoulder '.

l. 483. **hinc**, ' from this country '. **monstrata (est)**, ' there has been pointed out '.

l. 484. **Hesperidum.** The Hesperides were maidens who inhabited an island in the far west and possessed a garden of trees bearing golden apples, which were guarded by a serpent. Vergil calls this garden a **templum**.

epulasque. The -que is ungrammatical and can be dropped in translation.

l. 485. **sacros ramos**, i.e. on which the golden apples grew.

l. 486. It is not clear why the priestess should, as she appears to do, feed the guardian serpent with soporifics.

l. 487. **haec**, nom. sg. fem.

solvere, ' to free ', i.e. from love.

ll. 487, 488. **mentes quas velit**, ' what hearts she wills '. **velit** is subjunctive because dependent on the indirect statement se solvere. Cf. note on **dignetur**, l. 192.

l. 489. **sistere** and **vertere** depend on promittit se of l. 487.

fluviis is dative, but English looks at it in a different way and prefers to say ' of rivers '.

l. 493. **accingier** is an old form—and Vergil took pleasure in such—of the pres. infinitive passive, **accingi**. The construction of **accingier**, with me understood (with which **invitam** agrees) is acc. and infin., dependent on **testor** : ' that I apply myself unwillingly to '. Properly **accingo** means ' to fasten upon ', and its use in the passive voice, governing a direct object, **artes**, is an instance of the imitation of the Greek middle voice. For a note on this, cf. l. 137.

l. 494. **secreta**, adj. for adv., ' secretly '.

tecto interiore, ' in the inner palace '.

sub auras, ' up to the air ', i.e. ' towering high '. No doubt the pyre is visualised by Vergil as being built in an inner court, open to the sky—a feature of Mediterranean architecture.

l. 495. **fixa**, ' hung up '.

l. 496. **impius**, ' the wicked wretch '.

exuvias, ' his clothes '. **exuviae** are ' things stripped off ' and usually means spoils taken from a dead foe.

l. 497. **quo**, ' on which '.

superimponas. The jussive subjunctive, which means much the same as an imperative, superimpone.

l. 498. **iuvat monstratque sacerdos**, ' it is (my) pleasure to . . . and the priestess (so) commands (me) '.

l. 500. **novis . . . sacris**, ' hides death beneath these strange rites ', i.e. is causing a pyre to be built, not to rid herself by magic of her passion for Aeneas, but to destroy herself and burn thereon.

l. 502. **graviora,** *lit.*, ' worse things ', i.e. ' more dangerous consequences '.

morte, ' at the death ', abl. of time.

l. 504. Translate the abl. abs. **pyra erecta** by a ' when ' clause. For **sub auras** see note, l. 494.

l. 505. **ingenti . . . secta,** ' huge with pinewood pieces and sawn oak ', i.e. ' planks of oak '.

l. 506. **intenditque.** The **-que** = ' both ', and is unnatural in English.

fronde funerea. Examples of ' funereal greenery ' are the cypress and the yew.

l. 507. **super** is an adv.

exuvias. See note, l. 496.

l. 508. **effigiem.** Of Aeneas. Dido affects to believe she is bewitched by him, and can be cured magically by the destruction of his effigy.

toro. The marriage bed which is called **lectus** in l. 496.

futuri. A good example of the objective genitive, explained l. 188.

l. 509. **crines,** ' with loosened locks '; more literally ' having loosened her locks ', the passive participle **effusa** having the middle sense explained on l. 137.

l. 510. **ter centum deos,** ' (the names of) thrice a hundred gods '. The divinities mentioned all have associations with the nether world.

l. 511. **tria virginis ora Dianae,** *lit.*, ' the three faces of maiden Diana ', i.e. ' maiden Diana under her three forms '. The allusion here, and in **tergeminam Hecaten**, is to the identification of the two goddesses with one another and with **Luna** and Proserpine.

l. 512. **et,** ' also '.

simulatos (sc. esse) fontis, ' feigned to be from the Avernian spring '. Avernus, as the reputed entrance to Hades, would naturally furnish the appropriate ' holy water ' for rites in honour of the nether powers.

ll. 513, 514 describe the gathering of herbs for the contemplated magic rites. The nature of the herbs, the hour and the instrument of collection, are all important to the ritual. **messae** is from **meto**, and agrees with **pubentes herbae.**

l. 513. **et, '** too **'. ad, '** by **'.**

l. 514. The association of lac with **niger** is curious. Perhaps **niger** is not the colour of the liquid but of its ' dark ' effect. Say ' deadly '.

ll. 515, 516. These lines refer to a belief that a new-born foal had on its forehead a lump of flesh, which the mother removed immediately. If this piece of flesh were removed before the mother could do so, she took a dislike to her foal and refused to suckle it. The lump was called *hippomanes,* and was supposed to be efficacious in the preparing of love-philtres. Vergil calls it **amor** here, which may be translated ' charm '. **et** = ' also ', **nascentis, '** new-born ', and **equi, '** foal '.

l. 516. **matri,** dat. of disadvantage, common with compound verbs meaning ' to take away '.

ll. 517, 518. The queen offers sacrifice, and just as the gathering of herbs, described above, was subject to elaborate rules, so is her sacrificial dress prescribed. She approaches the altar with one foot bare and with her robe loosened.

l. 517. **mola.** Salted meal was sprinkled on the victims at sacrifice.

iuxta governs **áltaria.**

l. 518. **exuta,** middle use of passive voice, ' having freed '. See note on **circumdata,** l. 137.

l. 519. **moritura, '** resolved to die '.

ll. 520, 521. Order for translation is **tum precatur, si quod iustumque memorque numen habet curae amantes non aequo foedere,** *lit.,* ' then she prays, if any just and unforgetful divinity has for-a-care **(curae)** those-who-love **(amantes)** with compact not equal.' This is ' then she prays to whatever just and unforgetful power takes pity on unrequited lovers '. **habere aliquem curae**, ' to have someone for a care ' = ' to concern oneself with some-one '. **curae** is called predicative dative.

l. 523. **quierant** = quieverant, syncopated form, from **quiesco**.

l. 524. **cum**, ' (the hour) when '.

volvuntur, ' roll ' ; the Latin passive = English intransitive active.

l. 526. **quaeque**, ' both (those) which '.

l. 527. **tenent**, ' possess ', ' inhabit '.

somno positae, *lit.*, ' placed in sleep ', i.e. ' perched asleep '.

l. 529. **lenibant** = leniebant.

l. 530. **at non**. There is no verb, or rather we can understand **curas lenit** from l. 529.

animi, locative, as in l. 203.

Phoenissa, i.e. Dido.

l. 530. **solvitur in somnos**, *lit.*, ' is loosed into slumbers ', i.e. ' loses consciousness in sleep '.

l. 532. **aestu** = in aestu.

l. 533. **adeo** here need not be translated. It is occasionally used to emphasize the word it follows.

l. 534. **ago** must have the force here of **agam** : ' am I to do? '

inrisa, ' laughed at ', i.e. ' a laughing stock ', in apposition with the subject, ' I '.

l. 535. **experiar** and **petam** are deliberative subjunctives. See note on **agat**, l. 283.

Nomadum, ' with the Nomads '. Many relations between nouns are expressed by the genitive.

supplex, adj. for adv.

l. 536. ' though I have ere now **(iam)** so often scorned them as husbands.' As the relative clause contains a subjunctive, plainly with concessive meaning, we take **quos** as equivalent to **cum eos** and render accordingly.

l. 537. **ultima,** ' last ', **i.e.** ' uttermost ', obeying the Trojans in all things.

l. 538. **sequar,** deliberative subjunctive. See note, l. 283.

ll. 538, 539. **quiane,** etc. ' (Am I to do so) because it pleases (them) that they were relieved by my assistance before, and gratitude for (that) old act (of mine) stands fast (**bene**) in their mindful (hearts).'

Do I count on their gratitude, she means, to make me a welcome companion if I follow their destiny ? The question is ironical, as the following lines show.

l. 540. **fac velle** is for **fac me velle,** ' suppose me to be willing ', i.e. even if I were willing myself.

sinet, supply **ire** or some such infinitive.

ratibus. **in ratibus** in prose.

superbis is transferred epithet (hypallage). It is the Trojans, not their ships, that are proud.

l. 541. **invisam,** ' hated (as I am) '.

perdita, ' lost one ', i.e. ' poor soul '.

l. 542. **periuria,** ' treachery '.

l. 543. **fuga,** ' in flight '.

l. 544. **meorum,** ' of my (people) '.

l. 545. **inferar.** **inferor** here = ' carry myself on board ', i.e. ' embark ', the passive being equal as very often to active + reflexive pronoun object. **feror** is common for ' I go '.

vix. Dido means she had difficulty in persuading her subjects to make one migration, that from Tyre. They will hardly consent to a second.

quos . . . revelli. Take this clause after **rursus agam pelago.**

l. 546. **agam.** The object is **eos** understood, to which the preceding **quos** clause refers.

pelago, poetic dative for **in pelagus.**

l. 547. **quin,** ' nay, rather '.

morere, imperative of **morior**

l. 548. tu. Dido addresses these words to her sister, who is of course not present. Begin, ' It was thou, sister, who ', and translate the presents **oneras** and **obicis** by English perfects. **evicta** and **prima** agree with **tu**, **furentem** with me, object of **oneras** and **obicis**, understood. **furentem**, ' my mad heart '. **hosti** = Aeneas.

ll. 550, 551. ' It was not permitted (me) to lead a stainless (**sine crimine**) life, without part (**expertem**) in marriage, after the fashion (**more**) of a wild creature, and not to know such troubles.'

l. 552. servata, sc. **est. promissa**, ' given '.

fides. The pledge alluded to was that she would not marry again.

l. 553. rumpebat, ' did she bring bursting forth '. A strained use of **rumpo** which normally means ' break ' or ' burst '.

l. 554. certus eundi, ' sure of going ', **i.e.** ' resolved on departure '. **eundi** is gen. of the gerund.

l. 555. rebus paratis, abl. abs.

l. 556. huic, i.e. to Aeneas.

se obtulit, ' offered itself ', i.e. ' came '.

vultu, ' appearance '.

l. 558. omnia, ' in all things ', ' in all respects ', acc. of respect, and going closely with **similis**.

vocem, colorem, crines, membra are all in the same construction as **omnia** : ' in voice ', etc.

coloremque. The final **e** is elided before the **et** of the next line.

l. 560. nate dea, ' goddess-born ', i.e. ' son of a goddess '. **dea** is abl. of origin. Mercury is of course addressing Aeneas, whose mother was the goddess Venus.

ducere, ' prolong '.

l. 561. quae . . . pericula is indirect question, dependent on **cernis**.

deinde, ' in consequence ', i.e. of his delay.

l. 562. The Zephyri would be fair winds for a voyage from Carthage to Italy.

l. 563. **illa**, Dido.

dolos. The treachery she meditates is presumably her suicide, which is regarded as a betrayal of her sister and her subjects.

l. 564. **variosque, etc.,** ' and wakes the changeful tides of her wrath '. Her anger rises, then falls, then rises yet higher, like an incoming tide.

l. 565. **non fugis.** We should say ' Will you not flee? '

potestas, sc. est tibi, i.e. ' you have the power '.

l. 566. If he delays, Dido will have his fleet fired.

iam, ' soon '.

turbari trabibus, ' stirred up by (moving) ships '.

saevas, adj. for adv.

l. 567. **fervere flammis,** ' seething with flames ', i.e. ' a mass of flame '.

l. 568. **attigerit,** fut. perf., but English prefers the present, ' finds '.

Aurora was the goddess of the dawn.

l. 569. **heia, an** interjection, ' ho '.

age, like ' come ' in English, often precedes and draws attention to another imperative.

rumpe, *lit.,* ' break '. Say ' have done with '.

varium, etc., supply **est.** Notice the neuters **varium et mutabile,** ' a changeful and inconstant *thing*'.

l. 570. **se immiscuit,** ' mingled himself in ', i.e. ' vanished into '.

l. 573. **praecipites,** adj. for adv., ' swiftly '. **citi,** l. 574, is similar.

l. 574. **deus, etc.** Begin with **ecce iterum,** l. 576, ' lo, once again '.

l. 575. **incidere funes.** The funes are the mooring ropes and

Aeneas gives orders to cut them (incidere), since the normal process of casting off by loosing knots will take too long.

l. 576. instimulat, sc. nos.

l. 577. ovantes, adj. for adv., ' joyfully '.

ll. 578, 579. The subjunctives (jussive) are equal to imperatives. Adsis =' be nigh ', etc.

placidus, adj. for adv., and in a slightly unusual sense : ' graciously ' will serve.

et sidera, etc., ' bring into the heaven favouring stars ', i.e. to aid them in navigation.

l. 581. rapiuntque ruunt, ' they hurry and hasten '. rapiunt suggests swift operations with the hand, ' snatching ', at ropes, spars, oars, as does ruunt with the feet.

l. 582. deseruere, perf. So sudden is their quitting of the shore ; one moment they fill it, the next they have gone.

latet. The ships are so numerous that you cannot see the sea—hyperbole, poetic exaggeration.

l. 583. adnixi, (from adnitor) ' with might and main '. The word means ' striving '.

caerula, ' the blue ', i.e. ' the sea '.

l 584. prima, adj. for adv., ' first '.

l. 585. Tithoni. Tithonus was the husband of Aurora.

l. 586. Begin with ut primum. albescere, and procedere in the next line, may be rendered by pres. participles in English.

l. 587. aequatis, ' squared '.

l. 588. Supply esse. The order is, sensitque litora et vacuos portus esse sine remige.

remige = remigibus.

l. 589. percussa, and abscissa, l. 590, have the force of present participles active, and have as direct objects pectus decorum and flaventes comas respectively. Though perfect participles in form, they are used, like corresponding participles of deponent verbs, with present meaning. The construction, called the ' middle ' use of the passive voice, is explained in the note to circumdata, l. 137.

l. 591. **inluserit,** fut. perf., ' and shall he have mocked '.

l. 592. The subject, ' they ', of **expedient,** etc., **is** Dido's Carthaginians.

l. 594. **citi,** adj. for adv.

l. 597. **tum decuit,** supply **ea te tangere,** ' they should have touched you then '. **dabas,** ' offered '.

ll. 597, 598. **en dextra . . . quem,** ' Behold the pledge (**dextra**) and the plighted word (of him) whom . . .'. **eius,** antecedent to **quem,** must be supplied.

l. 600. **abreptum divellere** = **abripere et divellere.** When two finite verbs, or two infinitives, are required to be predicated of the same subject, the first of the two is usually expressed by a perfect participle passive in agreement with the object. Cf. **nuntium captum interfecerunt,** ' they caught and killed the messenger '.

l. 601. **absumere, and ponere,** l. 602, depend on **potui,** repeated from l. 600.

l. 602. **patriis,** ' his father's ', i.e. Aeneas '.

epulandum, *lit.,* ' to be feasted upon ', i.e. ' as a dish '. **epulandum** is gerundive and agrees with **Ascanium.** The serving as food of a murdered child to an ignorant father is a form of revenge recurrent in the Greek myths.

l. 603. **fuerat** is for **fuisset,** ' would have been '. Dido means an attack on Aeneas and his men might not have succeeded.

fuisset, past jussive, ' let it have been ', ' granted it had been so '.

l. 604. **metui,** ' had I to fear '.

moritura, ' being resolved to die '.

tulissem, ' I should have carried ', where ' should ' has the force of ' ought to '. The subjunctive is a past jussive, as are **implessem** and **exstinxem** in ll. 605, 606.

l. 605. **implessem** = **implevissem,** and **exstinxem, l. 606, exstinxissem.**

l. 606. **memet,** strong form of **me.**

ipsa, i.e. the bodies of her victims.

dedissem, ' should have thrown '. An original meaning of **do** is ' put '.

l. 607. **flammis**, ' with thy beams '.

l. 608. Dido recognizes in her tribulations the work of Juno. **nterpres et conscia**, ' instrument of these (my) troubles and **h**aving knowledge of them '.

l. 609. **nocturnis**, adj. for adv., ' by night '.

l. 609. **ululata**, *lit.*, ' howled '. Translate ' invoked with cries ' (Sidgwick). Hecate, a goddess associated with the underworld, was worshipped at cross-roads.

l. 611. **haec**, ' these words '.

meritum, adj. for adv., ' deservedly '.

malis, dat., ' to my wrongs '.

l. 612. **si**, etc. The order is, **si necesse est infandum (eius) caput tangere portus ac adnare terris**, the acc. and infin. **caput . . . terris** being dependent on **necesse est**. Begin, ' if it is inevitable (**necesse**) that . . .'.

l. 615. The first main verb is **imploret**, l. 617, ' let him beg for ' (jussive subjunctive, see note, l. 103). With the subject of this verb **vexatus** (615), **extorris** and **avulsus** (616) agree. **videat** (617), **fruatur** (619) and **cadat** (620) are jussives similar to **imploret**. The various items of this curse uttered by Dido are all fulfilled in due course, but not so painfully for Aeneas as Dido hoped.

bello et armis, *lit.*, ' war and arms ', say ' armed hostility '.

audacis populi. In the event an Italian tribe, the Rutuli, filled this role.

l. 620. make **inhumatus** into a verb ; ' and (lie) unburied '.

l. 622. **tum**, ' hereafter '.

stirpem, i.e. of Aeneas, ' his '.

l. 624. **populis**, ' between the nations ' of herself and Aeneas —Carthage and Rome.

sunto, 3rd pl. imperative of **sum**, ' let there be '.

l. 625. **exoriare** = **exoriaris**, jussive subjunctive, equivalent to an imperative.

aliquis, *lit.*, ' some '. Say ' unknown '. The ' avenger ' whom she adjures to arise is Hannibal.

nostris ex ossibus, ' from my bones ', which we express by ' of my flesh and blood '.

l. 626. **qui sequare**, ' to harry '. **sequare** = **sequaris** and is final subjunctive. **Qui**, as so often in final clauses, stands in place of **ut** + a pronoun (here, **tu**).

face ferroque, *lit.*, ' with torch and steel '. The English idiom is ' with fire and sword '.

ll. 628, 629. ' I invoke shore against shore (*lit.*, hostile to shore), wave against wave ', etc.

l. 629. **pugnent**, jussive. See note, l. 103.

l. 630. **partes in omnes**, ' in all directions '.

l. 631. **quam primum**, ' as soon as might be ', same construction as the common **quam celerrime**, ' as quickly as possible '.

l. 632. Dido asks the assistance of the old nurse of Sychaeus, since her own (l. 633) was dead.

l. 632. **Barcen**, acc. sg.

adfata, sc. **est**.

l. 633. **suam**, sc. **nutricem**.

patria, abl., of place where.

l. 635. **dic properet** would be in prose **impera ut properet**. **ducat** depends similarly.

l. 637. **veniat**, jussive.

The **vitta**, ' fillet ', was a ribbon tied round the head of persons about to offer sacrifice.

l. 638. **incepta paravi**, ' began and set in train '; cf. note, l. 600.

l. 639. **est animus**, ' it is my mind ', i.e. ' I am minded '.

finemque imponere curis is an example of dramatic irony.

The reader divines what Dido really means by these words; the nurse, of course, takes them in another sense.

l. 643. **aciem.** Translate by plural.

ll. 643, 644. **maculisque trementes interfusa genas,** *lit.*, ' sprinkled as to her quivering cheeks with spots ', i.e. ' with a mottled flush upon her quivering cheeks '. **genas** is accusative of respect.

l. 644. **pallida,** nom. **morte futura,** abl., ' at the approach of death '.

l. 645. **inrumpit,** ' bursts through '.

l. 646. **furibunda,** adj. for adv.

l. 647. **non hos . . . usus.** Translate in this order : **munus non quaesitum in** (for) **hos usus. munus** is accusative, in apposition to **ensem,** l. 646.

quaesitum. Apparently Dido had begged this sword as a keepsake.

l. 648. **hic,** adverb. **postquam,** ' when.'

l. 649. **lacrimis et mente,** ' in tears and thought ' (*lit.*, ' mind ').

morata, sc. **est.**

l. 651. **exuviae,** ' garments '.

dum fata, etc. Repeat **dulces,** ' sweet ', before **dum.**

l. 653. **vixi,** ' I have lived my life '.

Take **cursum** out of the **quem** clause. It is the object of **peregi.**

dederat. English prefers the simple past tense here.

l. 656. **ulta,** supply **sum.**

poenas recepi, ' I took back penalties ', i.e. ' I exacted retribution '.

l. 657. **felix,** supply **fuissem,** ' I should have been happy '.

tantum, adverb, ' only '.

l. 658. **carinae,** ' ships ', by synecdoche, as so often.

l. 659. **impressa,** middle use of passive voice, i.e. with active meaning, and with direct object, **os**.   See note on **circumdata**, l. 137.

moriemur, pl. for sg., and **moriamur**, l. 660, similarly.

l. 660. The double **sic** no doubt marks two blows with the sword.

sub umbras, ' down to the darkness '.

l. 661. **hauriat oculis**. The phrase **haurire oculis**, *lit.*, ' drink in with the eyes ', is Vergilian for ' gaze on '. **hauriat** is optative subjunctive, expressing a wish, ' may . . .'.

alto is adj. used as noun, exactly corresponding to English, ' the deep '.

l. 662. **Dardanus**, i.e. Aeneas. **et nostrae**, etc. To have seen Dido's blazing pyre will be an ill omen for the commencement of his Italian adventure.

ll. 663, 664. **media inter talia ferro conlapsam**, *lit.*, ' fallen by the steel amid such (words) '. Say, ' laid low, even as she speaks such words, by the sword '.

ll. 664, 665. **cruore spumantem**, ' spouting blood ', *lit.*, ' foaming with blood '.

l. 665. **it**, ' penetrates '.

l. 667. **femineo**. The final vowel is not elided.

l. 669. **non aliter quam si**, ' not otherwise than if ', i.e. ' just as if '.

immissis ruat hostibus, *lit.*, ' were falling, with (or owing to) the enemy rushing in ', i.e., ' were falling to the inrush of a foe '.

ruat. The subjunctive is always used in any clause making an imaginary comparison.

l. 671. **culmina** is governed by **per**, and has both **hominum** and **deorum** dependent on it.

l. 674. **per medios**, ' through the midst ', i.e. of the queen's attendants.

morientem agrees with **eam**, i.e. Dido, understood.

l. 675. hoc illud fuit, ' was it this? ', **i.e. ' was this thy** purpose? '

me fraude petebas, ' didst thou aim at me with deceit ', **i.e. ' didst thou seek to deceive *me*? '**

l. 676. All the emphasis is on the **hoc,** and can be preserved only by some such device as this : ' was this what that pyre of thine was preparing for me? '

l. 677. quid . . . querar, *lit.,* ' having been deserted, what am I to complain of first ', i.e. ' what complaint am I to put first in this, thy desertion of me? ' Anna means that her grievances are so many that she has difficulty in selecting the greatest. **querar** is probably deliberative subjunctive ; **see** note on **agat,** l. 283.

ll. 677, 678. comitemne sororem sprevisti, ' didst thou despise thy sister as comrade? ' i.e. ' didst thou reject thy sister's companionship? ' Anna reproaches Dido for not having planned the death of them both.

l. 678. vocasses, ' you should have called '. **vocasses** is past jussive. **tulisset,** l. 679, is similar, ' should have carried off '.

l. 680. struxi. The object must be ' this ', **i.e. the pyre,** understood.

l. 681. sic te ut . . . abessem, ' that, with you lying thus. I should be cruelly absent '. **crudelis** is nom in apposition.

l. 682. exstinxti, for **exstinxisti.** We should say, ' Thou hast destroyed, not thyself alone, but . . .'.

l. 683. date abluam. This is condensed. The sense is plainly ' give (me water that) I may wash therewith the wounds '.

ll. 684, 685. et extremus . . . legam, ' and that, if any last breath wanders above, I may collect (it) with my lips '. Anna means, to snatch a last kiss before death supervenes. Say ' that I may catch with my lips what dying breath still lingers there '.

l. 685. fata, from **for.**

gradus, i.e. the steps leading up to the pyre.

l. 686. **sinu,** ' with—but we say " to "—her bosom '.

amplexa, see note on **veritam,** l. 96.

l. 688. **illa,** Dido.

conata, in present sense, like **amplexa,** l. 686.

l. 689. **vulnus,** *lit.,* ' wound ', seems to be used, by Vergil's favourite avoidance of the obvious, for ' sword '. **stridit.** The point ' grates ' on the ribs as Dido moves her body.

l. 690. **sese** does double duty, as object, first of **attollens,** then of **levavit.**

l. 692. **caelo,** abl. of place where ; **in caelo** in prose.

reperta, abl., with **ea** (=luce) understood in the abl. abs. construction : ' when she had found it ', *lit.* ' it having been found '.

l. 694. **Irim.** Iris was the messenger of Juno.

obitus, pl. for sg.

l. 695. **quae resolveret,** ' to release ', **quae** being equal to **ut ea,** and **resolveret** final subjunctive.

l. 696. Take the second **nec** before **merita.**

l. 697. **misera,** adj. for adv.

l. 698. **illi.** The dative is, as very often, equal to an English possessive genitive, going with **vertice.** The line refers to the custom of cutting off a lock of a dead person's hair as an offering to Proserpina, wife of Dis and queen of the Underworld.

l. 699. **Orco.** Orcus is a name both for the Underworld and its god.

l. 700. **Iris.** The verb to this nominative is **devolat,** l. 702.

roscida, because Iris was the goddess of the rainbow.

l. 701. **adverso sole,** ' across the sun ', *lit.,* ' the sun (being) athwart ', abl. abs.

mille varios colores. See note on **roscida,** l. 700.

l. 702. **caput,** i.e. Dido's.

hunc, i.e. the lock of hair.

l. 702. Diti. Dis, or Pluto, was the god of the Underworld.

l. 703. iussa, ' (as I was) commanded '.

fero, ' I take '.

l. 704. dextra, sc. manu.

una, ' therewith ', i.e. with the cutting of the lock.

l. 705. dilapsus, sc. est.

in ventos, ' into the breezes of heaven '.

(In the following vocabulary only irregular verbs are given their principal parts in full. Otherwise the figures (1), (2), (3), (4) following a verb denote that it is a regular example of that conjugation. No conjugation number is given in the case of -io verbs like capio.)

ā, ab, *prep. with abl.*, from, by.

abeō, -īre, -iī, -itum, depart.

abluō, -ere, -uī, -lūtum (3), wash.

abnuō, -ere, -uī, (3), refuse

aboleō. -ēre, -ēvī, -itum, (2), destroy.

abripiō, -ere, -ui, -reptum, seize (600).

abrumpō, -ere, -rūpī, -ruptum, (3), break off, cut short (631).

abscindō, -ere, -scīdī, -scissum, (3), tear away, tear.

abscondō, -ere, -dī, -ditum, (3), hide.

absēns, -tis, absent.

abstulī, *see* auferō.

absum, -esse, āfuī, be away.

absumō, -ere, -sumpsī, -sumptum, (3), destroy.

ac, and.

accendō, -ere, -endī, -ēnsum, (3), inflame, fire.

accēnsus, *partic. of above*, fired.

accingō, -ere, -nxī, -nctum, (3), gird upon.

accipiō, -ere, -cēpī, -ceptum, receive ; hear (611).

ācer, ācris, ācre, keen ; fierce, high-spirited, (156).

acervus, -ī, *m.*, heap.

aciēs, -ēī, *f.*, eye, (643).

ad, *prep. with acc.*, to ; at, (62) ; near, (133).

adeō, -īre, -iī, -itum, visit, approach.

adeō, *adv.*, indeed, (96).

adfātus, -ūs, *m.*, address.

adfor (1 *dep.*), speak to.

adgredior, -ī, -gressus sum, (*dep.*), attack, assail.

adhuc, *adv.*, still.

adigō, -ere, -ēgī, -āctum, (3). drive ; hurl, (25).

adimō, -ere, -ēmī, -ēmptum, (3), take away.

aditus, -ūs, *m.*, access.

adloquor, -ī, -locūtus sum, (3 *dep.*), address.

admoneō, (2), admonish.

admoveō, -ēre, -mōvī, -mōtum, (2), move near.

adnītor, -ī, -nīxus sum, (3 *dep.*), strive ; lean on, (690).

adnō, (1), sail to (+*dat.*).

adnuō, -ere, -uī, -ūtum, (3), assent.

adquīrō, -ere, -quīsīvī, -quīsītum, (3), gain.

adsiduē, constantly.

adsiduus, -a, -um, constant.

adstō, -āre, -stitī, (1), come to rest, (702).

adsum, -esse, -fuī, be near, be present.

adsurgō, -ere, -surrexī, -surrectum, (3), rise, rise up.

advena, -ae, c., stranger.

adversor, (1 dep.), oppose.

adversus, -a, -um, opposite.

advertō, -ere, -tī, -sum, (3), turn towards; with animum understood, give heed.

aeger, -gra, -grum, sick.

Aenēās, -ae, m., Aeneas.

aēnus, -a, -um, adj., bronze, of bronze.

aequātus, -a, -um, reaching, (89).

aequō, (1), make equal; level.

aequor, -oris, n., sea.

aequus, -a, -um, equal.

aestus, -ūs, m., tide.

aetās, -ātis, f., age.

aeternus, -a, -um, everlasting, eternal.

aether, acc., -era, gen., -eris, m., upper air, sky; heaven (574, etc.).

aetherius, -a, -um, of the upper air.

Aethiops, -opis, m., Ethiopian.

Āfrica, -ae, f., Africa.

Āfricus, -a, -um, African.

Agamemnonius, son of Agamemnon.

Agathyrsī, -ōrum, m. pl., the Agathyrsi.

ager, -grī, m., field.

aggerō, (1), pile up; swell, (197).

agitō, (1), hound, hunt.

āgmen, -inis, n., column, troop, company, band.

āgnōscō, -ere, -nōvī, -nitum, (3), recognize.

agō, -ere, -ēgī, āctum, (3), drive; do; pursue, (465).

aiō, defective verb, say.

āla, -ae, f., wing; see note, l. 121.

ālātus, -a, -um, winged.

albēscō, -ere, (3), whiten (intr.).

aliēnus, -a, -um, foreign, (311).

aliquis, -quid, some-one, something; also aliquī, -qua, -quod, adj., some.

aliter, adv., otherwise.

alius, -a, -ud, other, another.

alō, -ere, aluī, altum, (3), feed, nurture.

Alpīnus, -a, -um, Alpine.

altāria, -ium, n. pl., altar.

altē, adv., deeply.

alter, -era, -erum, one or other (of two).

alternō, (1), hesitate.

altum, -ī, n., the deep, (310).

altus, -a, -um, high, tall, lofty; noble, (231).

amāns, -ntis, c., lover, (296, 370, etc.).

amārus, -a, -um, bitter.

ambiō, (4), go round.

ambo, -ae, -a, both.

āmēns, -ntis, distraught; aghast, (279).

āmittō, -ere, -mīsī, -missum, (3), lose.

amnis, -is, m., river.

amō, (1), love.

amor, -ōris, m., love; in pl., affections, (28).

amplector, -ī, -plexus sum, (3 dep.), clasp, embrace.

amplus, -a, -um, ample.

an, or; if introducing single question, not to be translated.

anceps, -ipitis, doubtful.

Anchīsēs, -ae, m., Anchises.

angustus, -a, -um, narrow.

anīlis, -e, of old age (lit., of an old woman).

anima, -ae, f., spirit, soul, life.

animus, -ī, *m.*, mind, heart, spirits.

Anna, -ae, *f.*, Anna.

annōsus, -a, -um, full of years.

ante, *adv.*, before ; earlier, (36).

ante, *prep.* +*acc.*, before.

anteferō, -ferre, -tulī, -lātum, put ... before ... (*with acc. and dat.*)

antequam, *conj.*, before.

antīquus, -a, -um, ancient, former.

aper, -prī, *m.*, wild boar.

apex, -icis, *m.*, peak.

Apollō, -inis, *m.*, Apollo.

aptō, (1), fit out, (289).

aptus, -a, -um, fit, fitted ; studded, (482).

apud, *prep.* +*acc.*, among.

aqua, -ae, *f.*, water ; flow, (489).

Aquilō, -ōnis, *m.*, north wind.

aquōsus, -a, -um, watery, rainy.

āra, -ae, *f.*, altar.

arbor, (arbos), -oris, *f.*, tree.

arcānus, -a, -um, secret.

ardeō, -ēre, arsī, arsum, (2), blaze.

ardor, -ōris, *m.*, eagerness.

arduus, -a, -um, steep.

arēna, -ae, *f.*, sand.

arēnōsus, -a, -um, sandy.

arguō, -ere, -uī, -ūtum, (3), show up.

arma, -ōrum, *n. pl.*, arms, weapons.

armō, (1), fit out, arm.

armus, -ī, *m.*, shoulder.

arō, (1), plough.

arrigō, -ere, -rēxī, -rēctum, (3), erect ; *pass.*, stand ; rise, (280).

ars, artis, *f.*, art.

artus, -ūs, *m.*, limb.

arundō, -inis, *f.*, reed ; arrow, (73).

arvum, -ī, *n.*, land, field.

arx, arcis, *f.*, citadel, tower.

Ascanius, -iī, *m.*, Ascanius.

aspectus, -ūs, *m.*, sight.

asper, -era, -erum, rough.

aspiciō, -ere, spēxī, -spectum, see, regard, watch.

ast (=at), but.

astrum, -ī *n.* star.

assurgō, -ere, -rēxī, -rēctum, (3), rise.

at, but ; yet, (615).

āter, -tra, -trum, black ; murky, dark (687).

Ātlās, -ntis, *m.*, Atlas.

atque, and, and moreover.

ātrium, -ī, *n.*, hall.

attingō, -ere, -tigī, -tāctum, (3), touch.

attollō, -ere, (3), raise, lift.

attonitus, -a, -um, dismayed.

auctor, -ōris, *m.*, founder.

audāx, -ācis, bold.

audeō, -ēre, ausus sum, (2 *semidep.*), dare.

audiō, (4), hear ; listen to, (439).

auferō, -ferre, abstulī, ablātum, steal away, take away ; withdraw, (389).

augur, -uris, *m.*, augur, (*one who foretells the future by interpreting omens*) ; *as adj.*, prophetic, (376).

aula, -ae, *f.*, court.

Aulis, -idis, *f.*, Aulis.

aura, -ae, *f.*, breeze ; air, (176, 278) ; light, (388).

aureus, -a, -um, golden.

auris, -is, *f.*, ear.

Aurōra, -ae, f., Aurora, (goddess of the dawn).

aurum, -I, n., gold.

Ausonius, -a, -um, Italian.

auspex, -icis, m., diviner (by the flight of birds); guide, (45).

auspicium, -I, n., auspice.

aut, or, either.

autem, but, however, moreover.

auxilium, -I, n., aid, help.

āvellō, -ere, -vellī, -vulsum, (3), tear away.

Avernus, -a, -um, Avernian, of Avernus.

āvertō, -ere, -tī, -sum, (3), divert, turn away; remove, (389, 394); destroy, (547).

avis, -is, f., bird.

avus, -I, m., grandsire.

axis, -is, m., vault (of heaven), (482).

bacchor, (1 dep.), move in frenzy (i.e., like a worshipper of Bacchus); rage, (666).

Bacchus, -I, m., Bacchus.

barba, -ae, f., beard.

Barcaeī, -ōrum, m. pl., Barcaeans, inhabitants of Barca.

Barcē, -ēs, f., Barce, nurse of Sychaeus.

bellum, -ī, n., war.

bene, adv., well.

bidēns, -ntis, f., sheep.

bis, twice.

Boreās, -ae, m., North Wind.

breviter, adv., briefly.

būbō, -ōnis, f., owl.

cadō, -ere, cecidī, cāsum, (3), fall; set, (480); die, (620).

caecus, -a, -um, blind; hidden, unseen.

caedēs, -is, f., slaughter.

caelum, -I, n., sky, heaven; weather, (53).

caerulus, -a, -um, blue.

callis, -is, m., path.

calor, -ōris, m., heat; warmth, (705).

campus, -I, m., plain.

candēns, -ntis, gleaming-white.

canis, -is, c., dog, hound.

canō, -ere, cecinī, cantum, (3), sing, sing of.

capessō, -ere, -sīvī, -sītum, (3), make for, seek, (346).

capiō, -ere, cēpī, captum, take, capture.

capra, -ae, f., roe-deer.

caput, -itis, n., head; chief, (640).

carbasus, -I, f., in pl., neut., carbasa, -ōrum, canvas; sail.

careō, (2), be without, lose (+abl.).

carīna, -ae, f., keel; often, ship.

carmen, -inis, n., song; spell, charm, (487).

carpō, -ere, -psī, -ptum, (3), pluck; consume, (2); enjoy, (522); snatch, (555).

Carthāgō, -inis, f., Carthage.

cārus, -a, -um, dear.

castīgō, (1), chide.

castra, -ōrum, n. pl., camp.

cāsus, -ūs, m., emergency, crisis, (560).

caterva, -ae, f., throng, troop.

Caucasus, -I, m., Caucasus.

causa, -ae, f., reason, cause.

cautēs, -is, f., rock.

celer, -is, -e, swift.

celerō, (1), quicken.

celsus, -a, -um, tall, high.

centum, *indecl.*, a hundred.

Cerēs, -eris, *f.*, Ceres.

cernō, -ere, crēvī, crētum, (3), see.

certāmen, -inis, *n.*, contention.

certō, (1), vie, (443).

certus, -a, -um, fixed, certain, sure ; resolved, (564).

cerva, -ae, *f.*, deer, hind.

cervus, -ī, *m.*, deer, stag.

Chaos, *n.*, Chaos.

chlamys, -ydis, *f.*, cloak.

chorus, -ī, *m.*, dance, (145).

cieō, -ēre, cīvī, citum, (2), wake ; call forth, (490).

cinctus, -a, -um, surrounded.

cingō, -ere, cinxī, cinctum, (3), surround, encircle.

cinis, -eris, *m.*, ash, ashes.

circum, *adv.*, *and prep. with acc.*, around, round.

circumdō, -are, -dedī, -datum, (1), put round.

Cithaeron, -ōnis, *m.*, Cithaeron.

citus, -a, -um, speedy.

clāmō, (1), shout ; call, (674).

clāmor, -ōris, *m.*, shout ; din, (303) ; cry, (665).

clārus, -a, -um, bright.

classis, -is, *f.*, fleet.

coepī, -isse, *def.*, began.

coeptus, -a, -um, begun ; half-built, (86).

coeptum, -ī, *n.*, purpose, intention, (642).

Cōeus, -ī, *m.*, Coeus.

cōgō, -ere, coēgī, coāctum, (3), compel, force ; shepherd, (289, 406).

colō, -ere, coluī, cultum, (3), cultivate ; tend, (458).

colōnus, -ī, *m.*, settler.

color, -ōris, *m.*, colouring, (558).

coma, -ae, *f.*, lock, hair, tress.

comes, -itis, *c.*, companion.

comitātus, -ūs, *m.*, train ; retinue.

comitor, (1 *dep.*), attend, accompany.

commisceō, -ēre, -miscuī, -mixtum (2), mingle.

commoveō, -ēre, -mōvī, -mōtum, (2), shake, wave, (301).

commūnis, -e, common.

compellō, (1), address.

complexus, -ūs, *m.*, embrace.

compōnō, -ere, -posuī, -positum, (3), put together, arrange.

concipiō, -ere, -cēpī, -ceptum, conceive.

concitō, (1) rouse.

concutiō, -ere, -cussī, -cussum, shake ; strike, (666).

condō, -ere, -didī, -ditum, (3), hide.

cōnfectus, -a, -um, enfeebled, (599).

cōnficiō, -ere, -fēcī, -fectum, accomplish.

cōnfīō, -fierī, *as pass. of* cōnficiō, (116).

cōniciō, -ere, -iēcī, -iectum, throw, shoot.

coniugium, -ī, *n.*, marriage.

coniunx, -ugis, *c.*, husband, wife.

conlābor, -ī, -lapsus sum, (3 *dep.*), collapse, fall.

conlūceō, -ēre, (2), gleam.

cōnor, (1 *dep.*), try.

cōnscendō, -ere, -scendī, -scēnsum, (3), mount.

cōnscius, -a, -um, sharing knowledge ; conscious, aware.

cōnsīdō, -ere, -sēdī, -sessum, (3), settle, sit.

cōnsilium, -ī, *n.*, design.

cōnsistō, -ere, -stitī, -stitum, (3), come to rest.

cōnspiciō, -ere, -spēxī, -spectum, see.

cōnsternō, -ere, -strāvī, -strātum, (3), strew.

cōnsulō, -ere, -suluī, -sultum, (3), consult.

contendō, -ere, -tendī, -tentum, (3), contend.

continuō, forthwith.

contrā, *prep. with acc.*, against; *adv.*, in answer, (107).

contrārius, -a, -um, hostile.

cōnūbium, -ī, *n.*, wedlock, union.

convectō, (1), carry.

conveniō, -īre, -vēnī, -ventum, (4), come together, assemble, gather.

convexus, -a, -um, curved.

convīvium, -ī, *n.*, banquet; company, (77).

cor, cordis, *n.*, heart.

cornū, -ūs, *n.*, horn.

corōna, -ae, *f.*, garland.

corōnō, (1), wreathe.

corpus, corporis, *n.*, body; creature, (523).

corripiō, -ere, -ripuī, -reptum, snatch.

crāstinus, -a, -um, to-morrow's.

crēdō, -ere, -didī, -ditum, (3), believe; confide, (422).

Crēs, Crētis, *m.*, a Cretan.

crēscō, -ere, crēvī, crētum, (3), grow, (*intr.*).

Crēsius, -a, -um, of Crete.

crētus, -a, -um, (*from* crēscō), sprung.

crīmen, -inis, *n.*, charge; guilt (550).

crīnis, -is, *m.*, hair, tress, lock.

croceus, -a, -um, saffron-hued, saffron, yellow.

crūdēlis, -e, cruel.

cruor, -ōris, *m.*, blood, gore.

cubīle, -is, *n.*, bed.

cubitus, -ī, *m.*, elbow.

culmen, -inis, *n.*, top, roof.

culpa, -ae, *f.*, fault.

cum, *prep. with abl.*, with.

cum, *conj.*, when, since.

cumulō, (1), heap up.

cunctor, (1 *dep.*), linger, hesitate

cunctus, -a, -um, all.

cupīdō, -inis, *f.*, desire, passion.

cupiō, -ere, -īvī, -ītum, desire, long, long for.

cūr, why.

cūra, -ae, *f.*, care; affliction, (1); pain, (332, 448).

cūrō, (1), care for.

cursus, -ūs, *m.*, course, running; voyage, (299); span, (653); haste, (672).

custōs, -ōdis, *c.*, guard, guardian.

Cyllēnius, -a, -um, Cyllenian, the Cyllenian, i.e., Mercury, (born on Mt. Cyllene); of Cyllene, (258).

Cynthus, -ī, *m.*, Cynthus.

Cytherēa, -ae, *f.*, Cytherea, a name of Venus, from the island Cythera, on whose shores she rose out of the sea.

damnō, (1), condemn.

Danaī, -um, *m. pl.*, Greeks.

Dardanius, -a, -um, Dardanian, (i.e., Trojan).

Dardanus, -a, -um, =*the foregoing*

Dardanus, -i, *m.,* Dardanus, (founder of Troy).

dē, *prep. with abl.,* down from, from ; about, concerning ; in, (153).

dea, -ae, *f.,* goddess.

dēbeō, (2), owe ; *in pass.,* be due, (276).

dēcēdō, -ere, -cessī, -cessum, (3), depart.

dēceptus, -a, -um, (*partic. of* decipiō), deceived.

dēcernō, -ere, -crēvī, -crētum, (3), resolve.

decet, (2 *impers.*), it is fitting.

dēclīnō, (1), droop.

decōrus, -a, -um, comely, lovely.

dēcurrō, -ere, -currī, -cursum, (3), run down ; speed down, (153).

decus, -oris, *n.,* beauty.

dēdīgnor, (1 *dep.*), disdain.

dēdūcō, -ere, -dūxī, -dūctum, launch, (398).

dēfendō, -ere, -endī, -ēnsum, (3), defend.

dēferō, -ferre, -tulī, -lātum, carry down ; report.

dēficiō, -ere, -fēcī, -fectum, swoon.

dēgener, -is, degenerate, base.

dēgō, -ere, dēgī, (3), spend, pass.

dēhiscō, -ere, (3), yawn, gape.

dēiciō, -ere, -iēcī, -iectum, throw down.

deinde, *adv.,* next, thereafter, then.

dēligō, -ere, -lēgī, -lectum, (3), choose.

Dēlos, -ī, *f.,* Delos.

dēlūbrum, -ī, *n.,* shrine.

dēmēns, -tis, out of one's mind, mad, insane ; madman, (562).

dēmittō, -ere, -mīsī, -missum, (3), send down ; admit, (428) ; *partic.,* dēmissus, hanging,(263).

dēripiō, -ere, -ripuī, -reptum, tear down ; cast loose, (593).

dēsaeviō, (4), spend one's wrath, (52).

dēscendō, -ere, -endī, -ēnsum, (3), descend, come down.

dēsecō, -āre, -cuī, -ctum, (1), cut off.

dēserō, -ere, -eruī, -ertum, (3), forsake, desert ; *partic.,* dēsertus, deserted, abandoned.

dēsinō, -ere, siī, -situm, (3), cease.

dēspiciō, -ere, -spēxī, -spectum, scorn.

dēstruō, -ere, -strūxī, -strūctum, (3), pull down, raze.

dēsuper, *adv.,* from above.

dētineō, -ēre, -tinuī, -tentum, (2), hold back ; hold, (85) (348).

dētorqueō, -ēre, -torsī, -tortum, (2) turn aside.

deus, -ī, *m.,* god.

dēveniō, -īre, -vēnī, -ventum, (4), come.

dēvolō, (1), fly down.

dexter, -tera *or* **-tra, -terum** *or* **-trum,** right ; favourable, (579)

dextera *or* **-tra, -ae,** *f.,* right hand.

dī, *nom. pl. of* deus.

Diāna, -ae, *f.,* Diana.

dicō, (1), devote, dedicate.

dīcō, -ere, -dīxī, dīctum, (3), tell, say.

Dictaeus, -a, -um, of Dicte (name of a mountain in Crete).

dīctum, -ī, *n.,* word.

Dīdō, -ōnis, *f.,* Dido.

diēs, -ēī, *m. or f.,* day ; time, (620, 697).

difficilis, -e, difficult.

diffugiō, -ere, -fūgī, scatter (intrans.) in flight.

diffundō, -ere, -fūdī, -fūsum, (3), spread abroad.

dignor, (1 dep.), think fit, deign.

dignus, -a, -um, worthy.

digredior, -dī, -gressus sum, (dep.), part.

dīlābor, -lābī, -lapsus sum, (3 dep.), slip away.

dīligō, -ere, -lexī, -lēctum, (3), love ; partic., dīlēctus, beloved.

dimoveō, -ēre, -mōvī, -mōtum, (2), move, move away.

Dīra, -ae, f., Fury.

dīrus, -a, -um, awful.

Dīs, Dītis, m., Dis, Ditis (a name of Pluto).

discernō, -ere, -crēvī, -crētum, (3) distinguish. See note on 264.

dissimulō, (1), hide.

dīva, -ae, f., goddess.

dīvellō, -ere, vellī, -vulsum, (3), tear apart; tear limb from limb, (600).

dīversus, -a, -um, different, various.

dīves, -itis, rich.

dīvidō, -ere, -vīsī, -vīsum, (3), divide.

dīvus, -a, -um, divine.

dīvus, -ī, m., god, (gen. pl., dīvum).

dō, dare, dedī, datum, give ; pay, (386) ; set, spread, (594) ; offer, (627).

doceō, -ēre, -cuī, -ctum, (2), tell, teach.

doleō, (2), grieve.

dolor, -ōris, m., grief ; agony, (693).

dolus, -ī, m., craft, guile, deceit ; treachery, (563).

dominus, -ī, m., lord.

domus, -ūs, f., house, home.

dōnum, -ī, n., gift.

dōtālis, -e, as a dowry, (104).

dracō, -ōnis, m., serpent.

Dryopes, -um, m. pl., the Dryopes, (a tribe in Greece).

dubius, -a, -um, wavering, (55).

dūcō, -ere, dūxī, dūctum, (3), lead.

dūctor, -ōris, m., chieftain.

dulcis, -e, sweet, pleasant ; dear, (493).

dum, while ; until, (325).

dūmus, -ī, m., thicket.

duo, -ae, -o, two.

duplex, -plicis, double.

dūrus, -a, -um, hard ; enduring, (247) ; stubborn, (428) ; cruel, (488).

dux, ducis, m.; leader.

ē or ex, prep. with abl., out of, from.

ecce, behold!

edō, edere or esse, ēdī, ēsum, (3), eat.

efferō, -ferre, extulī, ēlātum, raise.

efferus, -a, -um, maddened.

effigiēs, -ēī, f., effigy.

effor, (1 dep.), speak, speak out ; speak of, (456).

effundō, -ere, -fūdī, -fūsum, (3), loosen.

egeō, (2), be in need (+ abl.).

ego, meī, I.

ēgregius, -a, -um, surpassing, distinguished ; noble, (150).

ēiciō, -ere, -iēcī, -iectum, cast up.

Elissa, -ae, f., (a name for) Dido.

ēn, behold! lo!

Enceladus, -I, *m.*, Enceladus.

enim, *conj.*, for.

ēniteō, -ēre, -uī, (2), shine out.

ēnsis, -is, *m.*, sword.

ēnumerō, (1), recount, record.

eō, īre, īvī *or* iī, ītum, go, pass, move ; travel, (468).

epulae, -ārum, *f. pl.*, banquet ; food, (484).

epulor, (1 *dep.*), feast.

eques, -itis, *m.*, horseman, cavalier.

equidem, indeed ; for my part, (45).

equus, -I, *m.*, horse.

Erebus, -I, *m.*, Erebus.

ergō, therefore.

ērigō, -ere, -rēxī, -rēctum, (3), set up.

ēripiō, -ere, -ripuī, -reptum, snatch forth.

errō, (1), wander.

ēruō, -ere, -ruī, -rutum, (3), uproot, (483).

et, and, also, even, both.

etiam, too, also, even.

Eumenides, -um, *f. pl.*, (*name of*) the Furies.

ēvādō, -ere, -sī, -sum, (3), go out, mount, (685).

ēvānescō, -ere, -nuī, (3), vanish.

ēvincō, -ere, -vīcī, -victum, (3), vanquish.

ēvocō, (1), call forth.

ex, *see* ē.

exanimis, -e, distraught, (672).

exaudiō, (4), hear.

excieō, -ēre, -cīvī, -citum, (2), rouse (*partic.*, excitus, excited).

excipiō, -ere, -cēpī, -ceptum,

catch, rescue, succour ; rejoin, (114) ; divine, (297).

excubiae, -ārum, *f. pl.*, watch-fires.

exerceō, (2), practise ; pursue, (623).

exhauriō, -īre, -hausī, -haustum, (4), drain ; endure to the end, (14).

exigō, -ere, -ēgī, -āctum, (3), work out, plan.

exiguus, -a, -um, little.

exordium, -I, *n.*, beginning.

exorior, -īrī, exortus sum (4 *dep.*), rise, arise.

expediō, (4), make ready.

experior, -īrī, expertus sum, (4 *dep.*), try.

expers, -tis, without share in.

exposcō, -ere, -poposcī, (3), demand.

exquīrō, -ere, -quīsīvī, -quīsītum, (3), seek.

exscindō, -ere, -scidī, -scissum, (3), destroy.

exsequor, -ī, -secūtus sum, (3 *dep.*), carry out, perform, (421).

exsolvō, -ere, -solvī, -solūtum, (3), release.

exspectō, (1), await, wait for ; linger, (225).

exstinguō, -ere, -nxī, -nctum, (3) destroy.

exstruō, -ere, -ūxī, -ūctum, (3), build, rear.

exta, -ōrum, *n. pl.*, entrails, organs, vitals.

extemplō, forthwith.

exterreō, (2), terrify ; (*partic.* exterritus, appalled, terrified)

exterus, -a, -um, foreign.

extorris, -e, exiled.

extrēmus, -a, -um, last.

exuō, -ere, -uī, -ūtum, take off ;
     put off, drop, (319).

exuviae, -ārum, *f. pl.,* spoils.

facēssō, -ere, **-cēssī,** -cēssītum,
     (3), do eagerly.

facilis, -e, easy.

faciō, -ere, **fēcī, factum,** make, do.

factum, -ī, *n.,* deed, act.

factus, -a, -um, (*from* faciō),
     done.

fallō, -ere, **fefellī, falsum,** (3), de-
     ceive, cheat ; escape.

falx, -cis, *f.,* sickle.

fāma, -ae, *f.,* reputation, good
     name ; report, tale, rumour ;
     Rumour (*personified,* 173).

famula, -ae, *f.,* slave girl, maid.

famulus, -ī, *m.,* manservant.

fandō, *abl. of gerund of* **for.**

far, farris, *n.,* grain.

fas, *indecl.,* lawful.

fātālis, -e, granted by fate, (355).

fateor, -ērī, **fassus sum,** (2 *dep.*),
     confess.

fatīgō, (1), urge on.

fātum, -ī, *n.,* fate.

fātus, *perf. partic. of* **for.**

faux, -cis, *f.,* jaw ; *pl.,* **throat.**

fax, -cis, *f.,* torch.

fēlīx, -īcis, fortunate.

fēmina, -ae, *f.,* woman.

fēmineus, -a, -um, of women.

fera, -ae, *f.,* beast.

fērālis, -e, funereal, sinister,
     (462).

feriō, -īre, (4), smite.

ferō, ferre, tulī, lātum, bear,
     carry, bring, fetch, report.

ferōx, -ōcis, high-spirited.

ferrum, -ī, *n.,* iron, steel ; sword,
     (547).

fertilis, -e, fertile.

ferus, -a, -um, wild ; fierce, (466).

ferveō, -ēre *or* -ere, **-uī,** (2 *or* 3),
     seethe.

fessus, -a, -um, weary.

festīnō, (1), hasten.

festus, -a, -um, festal.

fībula, -ae, *f.,* brooch, clasp.

fictus, -a, -um, false.

fidēs, -eī, *f.,* belief ; faith, (373) ;
     pledge, (552).

fīgō, -ere, **-xī, -xum,** (3), fix ;
     wound, (70) ; *partic.,* **fixus,**
     fixed.

fingō, -ere, **-nxī,** -ctum, (3),
     mould, shape ; imagine, (338).

fīnis, -is, *m.,* end ; border, (211) ;
     in pl., boundaries, lands.

flāmen, -inis, *n.,* wind.

flamma, -ae, *f.,* flame, fire ; torch,
     (594).

flātus, -ūs, *m.,* blast.

flāvēns, -ntis, yellow, golden.

flāvus, -a, -um, yellow, golden.

flectō, -ere, **-xī, -xum,** (3), bend ;
     move, (35) ; lower, (369).

flētus, -ūs, *m.,* weeping.

flōrēns, -ntis, bright, (202).

flōs, -ōris, *m.,* flower.

fluctuō, (1), toss.

fluctus, -ūs, *m.,* wave.

fluentum, -ī, *n.,* stream ; *pl.,*
     waters, (143).

flūmen, -inis, *n.,* river.

fluō, -ere, **-xī, -xum,** (3), flow.

fluviālis, -e, river- (*as adj.*).

fluvius, -ī, *m.,* river.

foedō, (1), mar.

foedus, -a, -um, loathsome.

foedus, -deris, *n.,* treaty ; pact,
     (339).

fōns, -ntis, *m.,* spring.

[for] fārī, fātus sum (1 *dep.*,
defective), speak.
fore, *fut. inf. of* sum.
forma, -ae, *f.*, shape, form.
formīca, -ae. *f.*, ant.
forsan, *adv.*, perhaps.
fortis, -e, mighty, strong, brave.
fortūna, -ae, *f.*, fortune.
forus, -ī, *m.*, gangway (*of a ship*).
foveō, -ēre, fōvī, fōtum, (2), keep
warm ; cherish, (218) ; fondle,
(686).
frāter, -tris, *m.*, brother.
frāternus, -a, -um, a brother's.
fraudō, (1), cheat.
fraus, -dis, *f.*, deceit.
fremō, -ere, -uī, -itum, (3),
clamour, (146) ; resound, (668);
partic., fremēns, clamorous,
(229).
frēnum, -ī, *n.*, bridle ; bit, (135).
frētus, -a, -um, relying on, (+
abl.).
frīgidus, -a, -um, cold.
frondeō, -ēre, (2), be leafy ;
partic., frondēns, leafy.
frōns, -dis, *f.*, leaf ; leaves, (148) ;
foliage, greenery, (459).
frōns, -tis, *f.*, brow.
frūmentum, -ī, *n.*, corn.
fruor, -ī, (3 *dep.*), enjoy (+*abl.*).
frūstrā, in vain.
fuga, -ae, *f.*, flight.
fugiō, -ere, fūgī, fugitum, flee,
flee from ; shun, (389).
fulciō, -īre, fulsī, fultum, (4),
support.
fulgeō, -ēre, fulsī, (2), flash.
fulmen, -inis, *n.*, thunderbolt.
fulmineus, -a, -um, flashing (*like
lightning*).
fulvus, -a, -um, tawny, yellow.

fundāmentum, -ī, *n.*, foundation.
fundō, (1) lay the foundations of.
fundō, -ere, fūdī, fūsum, (3), pour ;
pour out, (621).
fūnereus, -a, -um, funereal.
fūnis, -is, *m.*, rope.
fūnus, -eris, *n.*, funeral ; death,
(308, 500, 618).
furiae, -ārum, *f. pl.*, madness,
(474).
furibundus, -a, -um, mad.
furō, -ere, -uī, (3), rage.
furor, -ōris, *m.*, madness.
fūrtīvus, -a, -um, clandestine,
(171).
fūrtum, -ī, *n.*, stealth.
futūrum, -ī, *n.*, what is to come,
the future.
futūrus, -a, -um, *fut. partic. of*
sum, future ; intended, (297).

Gaetulus, -a, -um, Gaetulian (*the
Gaetuli being an African tribe*).
Garamantis, -idis, *f.*, Garamantian
(*the Garamantes being an African tribe*).
gaudeō, -ēre, gāvīsus sum, (2
semi-dep.), rejoice ; rejoice in
(+*abl.*) ; *partic.*, gaudēns, glee-
fully, (190).
gelū, -ūs, *n.*, cold, frost.
geminus, -a, -um, twofold.
gemitus, -ūs, *m.*, sigh ; groan,
(667).
gemō, -ere, -uī, -itum, (3), sigh.
gena, -ae, *f.*, cheek.
genetrīx, -īcis, *f.*, mother.
genitor, -ōris, *m.*, father.
gēns, -ntis, *f.*, race, people.
genuī, *see* gignō.
genus, -eris, *n.*, kind, race, (40,
230) ; line, (365).

germāna, -ae, *f.*, sister.

germānus, -ī, *m.*, brother.

gīgnō, -ere, genuī, genitum, (3), beget.

glaciēs, -ēī, *f.*, ice.

gladius, -ī, *m.*, sword.

glomerō, (1), mass together.

glōria, -ae, *f.*, glory.

gradior, -ī, gressus sum, (*dep.*), stride.

gradus, -ūs, *m.*, step.

Graius, -a, -um, Greek; *as noun,* a Greek.

grāmen, -inis, *n.*, grass.

grandis, -e, great.

grandō, -inis, *f.*, hail.

grātia, -ae, *f.*, gratitude.

grātor, (1 *dep.*), congratulate (+*dat.*).

gravidus, -a, -um, pregnant.

gravis, -e, heavy, serious; sore, (1).

gremium, -ī, *n.*, lap.

Grȳnēus, -a, -um, Grynian.

habeō, (2), have, hold, keep.

haereō, -ēre, -sī, -sum, (2), stick, remain; cling to, (445); be fixed, (614).

hālitus, -ūs, *m.*, breath.

Hammon, -ōnis, *m.*, Ammon, (*name of an African god identified by the Romans with Jupiter*).

harēna, -ae, *f.*, sand.

harēnōsus, -a, -um, sandy.

haud, *adv.*, not.

hauriō, -īre, -sī, -stum, (4), drain.

Hecatē, -ēs, *f.*, Hecate.

hēia, ho!

herba, -ae, *f.*, grass; herb, (514).

hērēs, -ēdis, *m.*, heir.

hērōs, -ōis, *m.*, hero.

Hesperia, -ae, *f.*, Italy (' land of the evening, *or* west ').

Hesperides, -um, *f. pl.*, the Hesperides.

heu, alas!

hībernus, -a, -um, wintry.

hic, haec, hoc, this; he, she, it; they.

hīc, *adv.*, here.

hiems, -mis, *f.*, winter.

hinc, *adv.*, on *or* from this *or* that side; from this, (460).

homō, -inis, *m.*, man.

honōs *or* honor, -ōris, *m.*, honour; glory, (4); tribute, (207); veneration, (458).

hōra, -ae, *f.*, hour.

horrēns, -tis, rough.

horrendus, -a, -um, horrible, dreadful.

horreō, -ēre, -uī, (2), be rough; tremble at, (209).

horridus, -a, -um, bristling; dread, (378).

horrificō, (1), affright.

horror, -ōris, *m.*, fear, dread.

hospes, -itis, *c.*, stranger, guest.

hospitium, -ī, *n.*, hospitality.

hostis, -is, *c.*, foe.

hūc, *adv.*, hither, this way.

humerus, -ī, *m.*, shoulder.

humilis, -e, low.

hymenaeus, -ī, *m.*, marriage; *also in pl. with same meaning.*

Hyrcānus, -a, -um, Hyrcanian.

iactō, (1), toss about, harass, (14).

iam, *adv.*, now; any longer, (171).

iamdūdum, *adv.*, long since, now for a long time.

Iarbas, -ae, *m.*, Iarbas.

iaspis, -idis, *f.*, jasper.

idem, eadem, idem, the same.

ideō, *adv.*, therefore.

igitur, therefore.

ignārus, -a, -um, unaware.

igneus, -a, -um, fiery.

ignis, -is, *m.*, fire.

ignōtus, -a, -um, unknown.

īlex, -icis, *f.*, holm-oak.

Iliacus, -a, -um, Trojan.

ille, illa, illud, that ; he, she, it ; they.

illinc, *adv.*, from that side.

illūc, *adv.*, thither, that way.

imāgō, -inis, *f.*, face ; phantom, (353, 654).

imber, -bris, *m.*, rain.

immānis, -e, vast, monstrous.

immemor, -oris, unmindful.

immisceō, -ēre, -scuī, -xtum, (2), mingle in.

immittō, -ere, -mīsī, -missum, (3), send in ; implant (*with acc. and dat.*, 488).

immōtus, -a, -um, immoveable, immutable ; unmoved.

impellō, -ere, -pulī, -pulsum, (3), overthrow, (23) ; ply, (594).

imperium, -I, *n.*, command ; empire, (229).

impius, -a, -um, unholy ; mischievous, (298) ; unchaste, (596).

impleō, -ēre, -ēvī, -ētum, (2), fill.

implicō, (1), entwine.

implōrō, (1), beg for.

impōnō, -ere, -posuī, -positum, put; place ... on ... (*with acc. and dat.*).

imprecor, (1 *dep.*), pray, (629).

imprimō, -ere, -pressī, -pressum, (3), press ... on ... (*with acc. and dat.*).

improbus, -a, -um, wicked ; cruel, 412) ; *as noun,* villain, (386).

imus, -a, -um, lowest.

in, *prep. with acc.*, into, in, to ; *with abl.*, in ; within, (211).

inānis, -e, empty, vain ; little, (433).

incautus, -a, -um, all unwary.

incēdō, -ere, -cessī, -cessum, (3), move on.

incendō, -ere, -endī, -ēnsum, (3), set on fire, inflame ; *partic.*, incēnsus, blazing (*with passion,* 300).

inceptum, -I, *n.*, design, undertaking.

incertus, -a, -um, uncertain

incīdō, -ere, -dī, -sum, (3), cut.

incipiō, -ere, -cēpī, -ceptum, begin.

inclūdō, -ere, -sī, -sum, (3), shut in.

incomitātus, -a, -um, unaccompanied.

incubō, (1), lie on.

incumbō, -ere, -cubuī, -cubitum, lie upon ; set to work, (397).

indāgō, -inis, *f.*, encircling ; a ring of men, (121).

indignus, -a, -um, undeserved.

indulgeō, -ēre, -lsī, -ltum, (2), indulge ; give rein to, (51).

iners, -tis, cowardly, timid.

inexpertus, -a, -um, untried.

infabricātus, -a, -um, unwrought.

infandus, a, -um, inexpressible ; accursed, (613).

infectus, -a, -um, not done.

infēlix, -icis, unhappy.

infēnsus, -a, -um, hostile.

inferō, -ferre, -tulī, -lātum, carry onward, carry in.

īnfīgō, -ere, -xī, -xum, (3), fix, fix in.

īnflammō, (1), inflame.

īnflectō, -ere, -xī, -xum, (3), bend; sway, (22).

īnfrēnus, -a, -um, unbridled.

īnfundō, -ere, -fūdī, -fūsum, (3), pour on.

ingeminō, (1), be doubled.

ingemō, -ere, -uī, -itum, (3), groan.

ingēns, -tis, huge.

ingredior, -ī, -gressus sum, (dep.), begin, (107); move upon, (177).

inhiō, (1) gape; partic., inhiāns, with lips parted in eagerness (64).

inhospitus, -a, -um, inhospitable.

inhumātus, -a, -um, unburied.

iniciō, -ere, -iēcī, -iectum, throw on.

inimīcus, -a, -um, hostile.

inīquus, -a, -um, harsh, (618).

iniūria, -ae, f., wrong.

inlūdō, -ere, -sī, -sum, (3), mock, (with dat.).

innectō, -ere, -xuī, -xum, (3), weave.

inops, -opis, helpless.

inrīdeō, -ēre, -sī, -sum, (2), laugh at.

inrītō, (1), provoke.

inrumpō, -ere, -rūpī, -ruptum, (3), burst into.

īnsānia, -ae, f., madness.

īnsequor, -ī, -secūtus sum, (3 dep.) follow.

īnsīgnis, -e, conspicuous.

īnsistō, -ere, -stitī, (3), begin, (533).

īnsomnis, -e, sleepless.

īnsomnium, -ī, n., dream.

īnstaurō, (1), renew; begin, (63).

īnstimulō, (1), urge.

īnstō, -āre, -stitī, -statum, (1), press.

īnsuperābilis, -e, invincible.

intendō, -ere, -ndī, -nsum or -ntum, (3), stretch on; festoon, (506).

inter, prep. with acc., between, among; amid, (70).

intereā, adv., meanwhile.

interfundō, -ere, -fūdī, -fūsum, (3), sprinkle, mottle.

interior, -ōris, inner.

interpres, -etis, c., spokesman, messenger.

interrumpō, -ere, -rūpī, -ruptum, (3), interrupt.

intrō, (1), enter.

intus, within.

inultus, -a, -um, unavenged.

invādō, -ere, -sī, -sum, (3), attack.

inveniō, -īre, -vēnī, -ventum, (4), find.

invideō, -ēre, -dī, -sum, (2), begrudge.

invidia, -ae, f., envy.

invīsō, -ere, -vīsī, -vīsum, (3), visit.

invīsus, -a, -um, hateful.

invītus, -a, -um, unwilling.

invius, -a, -m, trackless.

Iovem, -is, -ī, -e, see Iuppiter.

ipse, -a, -um, -self.

īra, -ae, f., anger, rage.

Īris, -idis, f., Iris, (acc. Irim).

is, ea, id, that or this; he, she, it; they.

iste, -a, ud, that of yours; that; this of yours, (703).

ita, *adv.*, thus, so.

Italia, -ae, *f.*, Italy.

Italus, -a, -um, Italian.

iter, itineris, *n.*, journey, way.

iterum, *adv.*, again.

iubar, -aris, *n.*, beam.

iubeō, -ēre, iussī, iussum, (2), bid.

iugālis, -e, of marriage, marriage-
(*as adj.*).

iugum, -ī, *n.*, ridge ; slope, (147).

Iūlus, -ī, *m.*, Iulus.

iungō, -ere, -nxī, -nctum, (3), join.

Iūnō, -ōnis, *f.*, Juno.

Iuppiter, Iovis, *m.*, Jupiter.

iūrō, (1), swear.

ius, iūris, *n.*, law.

iussum, -ī, *n.*, bidding, command.

iustus, -a, -um, just.

iuventa, -ae, *f.*, youth, (*abstract*).

iuventūs, -ūtis, *f.*, youth ; *as
collective*, the young men, the
youth.

iuvō, -āre, iūvī, iūtum, (1), help ;
please, (538, 660).

iūxtā, *prep. with acc.*, beside ;
close to, (255).

labefaciō, -ere, -fēcī, -factum,
shake.

labō, (1), waver.

labor, -ōris, *m.*, work, trouble,
labour ; task, (233, 273).

lābor, -ī, lāpsus sum, (3 *dep.*),
glide ; fall, (318).

lac, lactis, *n.*, milk.

lacrima, -ae, *f.*, tear.

lacus, -ūs, *m.*, lake.

laena, -ae, *f.*, cloak.

laetus, -a, -um, joyful.

lāmenta, -ōrum, *n. pl.*, lamentation.

lampas, -adis, *f.*, torch.

Lāomedontēus, -a, -um, Trojan.

lapsus, -ūs, *m.*, course, (524).

lātē, far and wide.

lateō, -ēre, -uī, (2), lie hidden.

latex, -icis, *m.*, liquor.

Latium, -ī, *n.*, Latium.

latus, -eris, *n.*, side.

lātus, -a, -um, broad.

laus, -dis, *f.*, praise ; renown,
(233).

Lāvīnius, -a, -um, Latin.

lectus, -ī, *m.*, couch, bed.

lēctus, -a, -um, *see* legō.

lēgifera, (*f. of* lēgifer), the Law-
giver.

legō, -ere, -lēgī, lēctum, (3),
choose, gather, collect.

Lēnaeus, -a, -um, Bacchic.

lēniō, (4), soothe.

leō, -ōnis, *m.*, lion.

lētālis, -e, fatal, deadly.

lētum, -ī, *n.*, death.

levō, (1), relieve.

lēx, lēgis, *f.*, law, condition; term,
(618).

lībō, (1), pour in libation.

lībrō, (1), poise.

Libya, -ae, *f.*, Libya.

Libycus, -a, -um, Libyan, of
Libya.

licet, -ēre, -uit, (2 *impers.*), it is
allowed, it is permitted.

limbus, -ī, *m.*, border.

līmen, -inis, *n.*, threshold ; door,
portal, *very often*.

lingua, -ae, *f.*, tongue.

linquō, -ere, līquī, lictum, (3),
leave.

liquidus, -a, -um, flowing, (526).

litō, (1), perform *rites* acceptably.

lītus, -oris, *n.*, shore.

locō, (1), place, lay, set.

locus, -ī, *m.*, (*pl.*, locī *or* loca, *n.*), place.

longus, -a, -um, long.

loquor, -ī, locūtus sum, (3 *dep.*), speak.

lūctor, (1 *dep.*), struggle.

ludō, -ere, -sī, -sum, (3), play.

lūdus, -ī, *m.*, sport, game.

lūmen, -inis, *n.*, light; eye, (185, 244, 332, 369).

lūna, -ae, *f.*, moon.

lūstrō, (1), traverse, survey (607).

lustrum, -ī, *n.*, covert, brake.

lūx, lūcis, *f.*, light; life, (619, 631).

lūxus, -ūs, *m.*, extravagance.

Lyaeus, -ī, *m.*, (*a name of*) Bacchus.

Lycia, -ae, f., Lycia.

Lycius, -a, -um, Lycian.

lympha, -ae, *f.*, water.

māchina, -ae, *f.*, machine; crane, (89).

mactō, (1), sacrifice.

macula, -ae, *f.*, stain.

madeō, (2), be wet.

Maeonius, -a, -um, Asiatic.

maereō, (2), grieve.

maestus, -a, -um, sorrowful.

māgālia, -ium, *n. pl.*, huts.

magicus, -a, -um, magic.

magis, *adv.*, more.

māgnus, -a, -um, great.

māior, *comparative of* māgnus.

male, *adv.*, badly; *see note, l.* 8.

mālō, mālle, māluī, prefer.

malum, -ī, *n.*, (*neut. of* malus *used as noun*), evil, (169, 174); misery, (549).

malus, -a, -um, bad, evil.

mandātum, -ī, *n.*, command.

mandō, (1), instruct, (222).

mandō, -ere, -dī, -sum, (3), chew, champ, (135).

maneō, -ēre, mānsī, mānsum, (2), remain; still stand, (312, 343).

mānēs, -ium, *m. pl.*, spirit, spirits; shade, shades.

manica, -ae, *f.*, sleeve.

manifestus, -a, -um, full, plain (358).

manus, -ūs, *f.*, hand; company, (544).

mare, -is, *n.*, sea.

marītus, -ī, *m.*, husband.

marmor, -oris, *n.*, marble.

marmoreus, -a, -um, of marble, marble- (*as adjective*).

Mārs, -tis, *m.*, Mars.

Mārtius, -a, -um, of Mars, martial.

Massȳlus, -a, -um, Massylian; African, (*since the Massylians were an African tribe*)

māter, -tris, *f.*, mother.

māternus, -a, -um, a mother's, maternal.

Maurūsius, -a, -um, Moorish.

māximus, -a, -um, *superlative of* māgnus.

mēcum, with me.

meditor, (1 *dep.*), contemplate.

medius, -a, -um, mid, middle of.

medulla, -ae, *f.*, marrow.

mel, mellis, *n.*, honey.

melior, *comparative of* bonus.

membrum, -ī, *n.*, limb.

mēmet, *strengthened form of* mē.

meminī, meminisse, *defective vb.* remember (*with gen.*, 335).

memor, -oris, mindful.

memorābilis, -e, memorable.

memorō, (1), mention.

mēne = me + ne, *interrogative suffix.*

mēns, -ntis, *f.*, mind ; purpose,
(449, 595).

mēnsa, -ae, *f.*, table, course.

mentum, -ī, *n.*, chin.

Mercurius, -ī, *m.*, Mercury.

mereō, (2), deserve.

mereor, (2 *dep.*), deserve.

meritum, -ī, *n.*, service.

meritus, -a, -um, deserved, (611,
696).

messus, *from* metō.

metō, -ere, messuī, messum, (3),
reap, cut.

metuō, -ere, -uī, -ūtum, (3), fear.

metus, -ūs, *m.*, fear.

meus, -a, -um, my.

migrō, (1), be on the move.

mīlle, a thousand, (*adj.*).

mināe, -ārum, *f. pl.* menaces,
threats.

mīrābilis, -e, wonderful.

mīrus, -a, -um, wondrous.

misceō, -ēre, -cuī, -xtum *or*
-stum, (2), mingle, mix.

miser, -era, -erum, hapless.

miserābilis, -e, pitiable, piteous.

misereor, (2 *dep.*), pity (+ *gen.*).

miseror, (1 *dep.*), take pity on.

mitra, -ae, *f.*, ribbon.

mittō, -ere, mīsī, missum, (3),
send ; place, (231).

mixtus, *see* misceō.

Mnestheūs, -eī, *m.*, Mnestheus.

mōbilitās, -tātis, *f.*, quickness.

modo, *adv.*, only.

modus, -ī, *m.*, limit ; end, (98) ;
method, means, (294, 475).

moenia, -ium, *n. pl.*, walls.

mola, -ae, *f.*, meal.

mōlior, (4 *dep.*), labour at.

mollis, -e, soft, easy.

moneō, (2), admonish.

monimentum, -ī, *n.*, reminder.

monitum, -ī, *n.*, warning, (331).

monitus, -ūs, *m.*, warning.

mōns, montis, *m.*, mountain.

mōnstrō, (1) point out, show ;
prescribe, (636).

mōnstrum, -i, *n.*, monster.

mora, -ae, *f.*, delay.

moribundus, -a, -um, dying,
doomed to die.

morior, -ī, mortuus sum, (*dep.*),
die.

moror, (1 *dep.*), delay, linger.

mors, mortis, *f.*, death.

mortālis, -e, mortal.

mōs, mōris, *m.*, custom.

mōtus, -ūs, *m.*, movement.

moveō, -ēre, mōvī, mōtum, (2),
move.

mox, *adv.*, soon, presently.

mūgiō, (4), groan, (490).

multiplex, -icis, various.

multus, -a, -um, much ; great,
(3).

mūnus, -eris, *n.*, gift.

mūrex, -icis, *m.*, purple (*actually
a shell-fish from which the dye
was extracted*).

murmur, -uris, *n.*, rumbling, (160)

mūrus, -ī, *m.*, wall.

mūtābilis, -e, changeable, inconstant.

mūtō, (1), change.

nam, *conj.*, for.

namque, *conj.*, for.

nārrō, (1), relate.

nāscor, -ī, nātus sum, (3 *dep.*), be
born.

natō, (1), swim ; float, (398).

nātus, -ī, m., son (partic. of nāscor, 605).

nauta, -ae, m., sailor.

nāvāle, -is, n., dock, dockyard.

nāvigō, (1), sail.

nāvis, -is, f., ship.

-ne, interrogative suffix.

nē, not, that . . . not.

nec, see neque.

necdum, and . . . not yet.

necesse, indecl., inevitable.

nectō, -ere, nexuī, nexum, (3), fasten.

nefandus, -a, -um, impious.

nefas, indecl., n., crime, (306, 563).

negō, (1), deny.

nēmō, nūllīus, no one.

nemus, -oris, n., forest.

nepōs, -ōtis, m., grandson ; grandchild, descendant.

neque, or nec, neither, nor ; and not.

nēquīquam, adv., in vain.

nesciō, (4) not know, be in ignorance.

nescius, -a, -um, unaware, not knowing.

nexus, partic. of nectō, convulsed, (695).

niger, -gra, -grum, black.

nigrāns, -ntis, black.

nigrescō, -ere, -gruī, (3), go black.

nihil or nīl, nothing, indecl.

nimbus, -ī, m., storm cloud.

nimium, too.

nītor, -ī, nīxus or nīsus sum, (3 dep.), strive ; lean.

niveus, -a, -um, snow-white.

nix, nivis, f., snow.

nocturnus, -a, -um, by night, night- (as adj.).

nōdō, (1), knot.

Nomās, -adis, m., Nomad, Numidian.

nōmen, -inis, n., name.

nōn, not.

nōndum, adv., not yet.

nōrās, nōris = nōverās, nōveris, from nōscō.

nōscō, -ere, nōvī, nōtum, (3) learn ; in perf. tenses, know.

noster, -tra, -trum, our ; often, my.

nōtus, -a, -um, familiar, (648).

novō, (1), commence ; change.

novus, -a, -um, new ; strange, (500) ; in superlative, last (650).

nox, -ctis, f., night, darkness.

nūbēs, -is, f., cloud.

nūbilus, -a, -um, cloudy ; neuter, nūbilum, as noun, cloud.

nūllus, -a, -um, no ; as pron., no-one, (456).

num, whether (in indirect questions) ; for num, in direct questions, see note ll. 369, 370).

nūmen, -inis, n., power, presence, will, (of a god) ; divinity, (382).

Numida, -ae, m., a Numidian.

numquam, adv., never.

nunc, adv., now.

nūntia, -ae, f., (female) messenger.

nūntius, -ī, m., news.

nusquam, adv., nowhere.

nūtō, (1), nod.

nūtrīx, -īcis, f., nurse, foster-mother.

nympha, -ae, f., nymph.

ō, oh!

obiciō, -ere, -iēcī, -iectum, expose.

obitus, -ūs, m., passing, (= death).

oblītus, -a, -um, (partic. of oblīviscor), forgetful.

oblīvīscor, -ī, oblītus sum, (3),
forget (+gen.).

obmūtēscō, -ere, -uī, (3), be struck
dumb.

obnītor, -ī, -nīxus sum, (3 dep.),
struggle against, thrust against,
(406).

oborior, -īrī, -ortus sum, (4 dep.),
rise.

obscēnus, -a, -um, loathsome.

obscūrus, -a, -um, dark.

obstō, -āre, -stitī, -statum, (1),
stand in the way (of).

obstruō, -ere, -xī, -ctum, (3), stop
up.

occupō, (1), seize ; spread over,
(499).

ōceanus, -ī, m., ocean.

ōcius, adv., swiftly.

oculus, -ī, m., eye.

ōdī, -isse, def., hate.

odium, -ī, n., hatred.

odōrus, -a, -um, keen-scented.

offerō, -ferre, -tulī, -lātum, bring in
the way ; sē offerre, appear,
(557).

ōlim, adv., hereafter, (627).

olle, = ille, (105).

Olympus, -ī, m., Olympus.

ōmen, -inis, n., omen.

omnīnō, adv., utterly.

omnipotēns, -ntis, almighty, all-
powerful.

omnis, -e, all.

onerō, (1), load.

opācus, -a, -um, impenetrable.

operiō, -īre, -ruī, -rtum, (4),
cover.

opem, opis, (no nom.), aid ; in pl.,
wealth.

optātus, -a, -um, (partic. of optō),
longed for.

optimus, -a, -um, superl. of
bonus, excellent.

optō, (1), wish, choose, pray.

opus, -eris, n., work, toil ; deed,
(607).

ōra, -ae, f., shore.

orbis, -is, m., world.

Orcus, -ī, m., Orcus.

Orestes, -is, m., Orestes.

orgia, -ōrum, n. pl., festival,
orgies.

Ōrīon, -onis, m., Orion.

ornus, -i, f., ash-tree.

ōrō, (1), pray, pray for.

ortus, -ūs, m., rising.

ōs, ōris, n., mouth, face ; looks,
(329) ; form, (511) ; in pl.,
often, lips.

os, ossis, n., bone.

ostendō, -ere, -ndī, -ntum, (3),
show.

ostentō, (1), show.

ostrum, -ī, n., purple.

ōtium, -ī, n., leisure.

ovīle, -is, n., sheepfold.

ovō, (1), cheer.

pacīscor, -ī, pactus sum, (3 dep.),
make a compact.

pactus, -a, -um, (partic. of foregoing in pass. sense), plighted.

pallēns, -ntis, pale.

pallidus, -a, -um, pale.

pallor, -ōris, m., paleness.

papāver, -eris, n., poppy.

pār, paris, equal ; even.

parātus, -a, -um, ready.

parēns, -ntis, c., parent ; mother
or father.

pāreō, (2), obey (+dat.).

Paris, -idis, m., Paris.

pariter, *adv.*, alike, together.

parō, (1), prepare, make ready; prepare for, (299); proceed with, (88); carry out, (503).

pars, -rtis, *f.*, part; quarter, (153).

parvulus, -a, -um, little, tiny.

parvus, -a, -um, small.

passim, *adv.*, in all directions.

pāstor, -ōris, *m.*, shepherd.

pateō, -ēre, -uī, (2) lie open; *partic.*, patēns, open.

pater, -tris, *m.*, father; *in pl.*, elders, (682).

patera, -ae, *f.*, bowl.

patior, -ī, passus sum, (*dep.*), suffer, allow.

patria, -ae, *f.*, homeland.

patrius, -a, -um, of one's country.

paucī, -ae, -a, few.

paulum, *adv.*, a little.

pāx, pācis, *f.*, peace.

pectus, -oris, *n.*, breast, heart, bosom.

pecus, -oris, *n.*, herd.

pecus, -udis, *f.*, beast.

pelagus, -ī, *n.*, sea.

penātēs, -ium, *m. pl.*, household gods.

pendeō, -ēre, pependī, (2), hang; hang fire, (88).

penetrālis, -e, interior, (504).

penna, -ae, *f.*, wing.

Pentheūs, -eī, *m.*, Pentheus.

per, *prep. with acc.*, through, throughout, over.

peragō, -ere, -ēgī, -āctum, (3), carry out, complete.

peragrō, (1), wander through.

percutiō, -ere, -cussī, -cussum, beat.

perditus, -a, -um, lost, ruined.

perdō, -ere, -didī, -ditum, (3), lose.

pereō, -īre, -īvī or iī, -itum, be lost, perish.

pererrō, (1), wander over.

perferō, -ferre, -tulī, -lātum, endure.

perficiō, -ere, -fēcī, -fectum, complete.

perfidus, -a, -um, treacherous, forsworn; *as noun*, traitor, (305, 366, 421).

Pergama, -ōrum, *n. pl.*, Pergama, (*citadel of Troy*).

pergō, -ere, -rēxī, -rēctum, (3), proceed, go on.

perhibeō, (2), say, tell.

perīculum, -ī, *n.*, danger.

periūrium, -ī, *n.*, falsehood.

permittō, -ere, -mīsī, -missum, (3), entrust; commit, (640).

pernīx, -īcis, swift.

perpetuus, -a, -um, unbroken.

persentiō, -īre, -nsī, -nsum, (4), perceive, feel deeply.

pertaedet, -ēre, -uit or -sum est, (2 *impers.*), it wearies.

pēs, pedis, *m.*, foot.

pestis, -is, *f.*, plague, sickness.

petō, -ere, -īvī, -ītum, (3), seek; request.

pharetra, -ae, *f.*, quiver.

Phoebēus, -a, -um, of Phoebus *or* Apollo.

Phoebus, -ī, *m.*, Phoebus, (*name of* Apollo).

Phoenissa, -ae, *f.*, Phoenician.

Phrygius, -a, -um, Trojan.

Phryx, -ygis, *m.*, a Trojan.

piāculum, -ī, *n.*, victim, (636).

pictus, -a, -um, embroidered, (137, 206); tattooed, (146); bright, (525).

piget, -ēre, -uit (2 *impers.*), it dis-
gusts.

pinguis, -e, rich.

pīnifer, -era, -erum, pine-clad.

piscōsus,-a,-um, teeming with fish.

pius, -a, -um, dutiful, righteous ;
good, (393) ; holy, (464, 637).

placeō, (2), please (+*dat.*).

placidus, -a, -um, peaceful, (5,
522) ; calm.

plaga, -ae, *f.*, toils, hunting-net.

plangor, -ōris, *m.*, lamentation.

planta, -ae, *f.*, sole (*of foot*).

plūma, -ae, *f.*, feather.

plūrimus, -a, -um, most, very
much.

poena, -ae, *f.*, penalty, punishment.

Poenus, -a, -um, Carthaginian.

polus, -ī, *m.*, sky, heaven.

pōnō, -ere, -suī, -situm, (3), place,
put ; build, (200, 202, 344).

populō, (1), plunder.

populus, -ī, *m.*, people, nation.

porta, -ae, *f.*, gate.

portō, (1), carry.

portus, -ūs, *m.*, harbour.

poscō, -ere, poposcī, (3), ask,
demand.

possum, posse, potuī, can, be able.

post, *prep. with acc.*, after ; since,
(20).

post, *adv.*, after, afterwards.

posterus, -a, -um, next ; *fem.*,
postera, the next day, (6).

postquam, after, when, since.

potestās, -ātis, *f.*, power.

potior, -us, preferable.

potius, *adv.*, rather.

potior, (4 *dep.*), gain possession
of, (+*abl.*).

praeceps, -ipitis, headlong.

praecipitō, (1), stream, (251) ;
hasten away.

praeclārus, -a, -um, famous.

praeda, -ae, *f.*, booty.

praedictum, -ī, *n.*, prophecy.

praemium, -ī, *n.*, reward.

praeripiō, -ere, -ripuī, -reptum,
snatch.

praesentiō, -īre, -ēnsī, -ēnsum, (4),
be early aware of.

praetendō, -ere, -ndī, -ntum, (3),
offer.

praetereā, *adv.*, moreover.

praetereō, -īre, -īvī *or* -iī, -itum,
pass, outstrip.

praetexō, -ere, -xuī, -xtum, (3),
disguise, hide.

prāvus, -a, -um, crooked, vicious.

precem, -is, *f.*, (*no nom.*), entreaty.

precor, (1 *dep.*), pray, entreat.

premō, -ere, pressī, pressum, (3),
press ; suppress, fight down,
(232).

pretium, -ī, *n.*, price.

Priamus, -ī, *m*., Priam.

prīmō, *adv.*, at first.

prīmum, *adv.*, first.

prīmus, -a, -um, first.

principiō, *adv.*, first.

prior, -us, former.

prius, *adv.*, before, sooner.

prō, *prep. with abl.*, in accordance
with.

prō, *interjection*, oh!

probō, (1), approve.

prōcēdō, -ere, -cessī, -cessum, (3),
advance.

procul, *adv.*, afar, far.

procus, -ī, *m.*, suitor.

prōdō, -ere, -didī, -ditum, (3),
betray ; father, (231).

proficīscor, -ī, profectus sum, (3 *dep.*), set out.

[profor], -fārī, -fātus sum, (1 *dep.*, *defect.*), speak out.

profundus, -a, -um, deep.

prōgīgnō, -ere, -genuī, -genitum, (3), produce.

prōgredior, -ī, -gressus sum, (*dep.*), go *or* come forth.

prōles, -is, *f.*, posterity, (236); child.

prōmereor, (2 *dep.*), deserve.

prōmittō, -ere, -mīsī, -missum, (3), promise.

prōnuba, -ae, *f.*, bride's attendant, (*by Roman custom, a matron*).

properō, (1), make haste, hasten.

proprius, -a, -um, own.

propter, *prep. with acc.*, on account of.

prōpūgnāculum, -ī, *n.*, battlement.

Prōserpina, -ae, *f.*, Proserpine.

prōspiciō, -ere, -spēxī, -spectum, perceive, (410).

prōtinus, *adv.*, forthwith.

proximus, -a, -um, nearest, next.

pūbēns, -ntis, young.

pudor, -ōris, *m.*, shame, modesty; chastity, (27); scruples, (55).

puer, -ī, *m.*, boy.

pūgna, -ae, *f.*, fight.

pūgnō, (1), fight.

pūgnus, -ī, *m.*, fist.

pulcher, -chra, -chrum, beautiful, fair, handsome.

pulsō, (1), buffet.

pulverulentus, -a, -um, dusty.

Pūnicus, -a, -um, Punic, Carthaginian.

puppis, -is, *f.*, stern (*of ship*); *often*, ship.

purpureus, -a, -um, purple.

Pygmalion, -ōnis, *m.*, Pygmalion.

pyra, -ae, *f.*, pyre, funeral pile.

quaerō, -ere, -sīvī, -sītum, (3), seek, search (for); beg, (647).

quālis, -e, of such a kind as; such as; as; like.

quam, *adv.*, how; *after* tam, as.

quam, *conj.*, than.

quamquam, *conj.*, although.

quandō, *conj.*, since, (*causal*), (291, 315).

quantus, -a, -um, how great; as great as; as.

quassō, (1), batter.

quater, *adv.*, four times.

-que, and.

quercus, -ūs, *f.*, oak.

querēla, -ae, *f.*, complaint.

queror, -ī, questus sum, (3), complain.

questus, -ūs, *m.*, complaint, lament.

quī, quae, quod, *rel. pron.*, who, which, that; *interrog. adj.*, what, which.

quia, *conj.*, because.

quīcunque, quaecunque, quodcunque, whoever, whatever.

quid, why. *See also* quis.

quiēs, -ētis, *f.*, repose, sleep.

quiescō, -ere, -ēvī, -ētum, (3), grow still.

quiētus, -a, -um, quiet.

quīn, *conj.*, why not, (99); nay, (309).

quippe, *adv.*, forsooth.

quis, quid, *interrog. pron.*, who, what.

quis, quid, *indef. pron.*, any one, anything ; someone, something.

quisquam, quicquam *or* **quidquam,** anyone, anything, (*in negative or virtually negative sentences*).

quisquis, quicquid *or* **quidquid,** whoever, whatever.

quō, *adv.*, whither ; to what purpose, (98) ; in order that, (106, 452).

quondam, *adv.*, formerly ; before, (35) ; once, (307).

quoniam, *conj.*, since.

quoque, *adv.*, also.

quot, how many ; as many as ; as.

quotiēns (quotiēs), *conj.*, as often as, whenever.

rabiēs, -ēī, *f.*, rage, madness.

radius, -ī, *m.*, ray.

rādīx, -īcis, *f.*, root.

rāmus, -ī, *m.*, bough.

rapidus, -a, -um, swift.

rapiō, -ere, -puī, -ptum, seize, ravish, ; hurry, (286).

raptum, -ī, *m.*, plunder.

rārus, -a, -um, fine (*applied to nets, of wide mesh or thin cord*).

ratiō, -ōnis, *f.*, way, means.

ratis, -is, *f.*, raft ; ship, (53, 540, 593).

recēdō, -ere, -cessī, -cessum, (3), flee, (705).

recidīvus, -a, -um, restored, resurrected, (344).

recingō, -ere, -nxī, -nctum, (3), loosen.

recipiō, -ere, -cēpī, -ceptum, take back ; receive, (214, 236).

reclūdō, -ere, -sī, -sum, (3), open ; unsheathe, (646).

recursō, (1), run back, recur.

reddō, -ere, -didī, -ditum, (3), give back.

redeō, -īre, -īvī, *or* **iī, -itum,** return.

redūcō, -ere, -xī, -ctum, (3), bring back.

refellō, -ere, -fellī, (3), refute.

referō, -ferre, -tulī, -lātum, bear back ; answer, (31) ; recall, (329) ; report again.

rēgīna, -ae, *f.*, queen.

regiō, -ōnis, *f.*, region.

rēgius, -a, -um, royal.

rēgnātor, -ōris, *m.*, king, ruler.

rēgnum, -ī, *n.*, kingdom, realm.

regō, (3), rule.

relictus, -a, -um, abandoned.

relinquō, -ere, -līquī, -lictum, (3), leave ; abandon (432).

reliquiae, -ārum, *f. pl.*, relics, (343).

rēmex, -igis, *m.*, rower.

remittō, -ere, -mīsī, -missum, (3), send back ; repay (436).

rēmus, -ī, *m.*, oar.

reor, -rērī, ratus sum, (2 *dep.*), think.

repellō, -ere, reppulī, -pulsum, (3), reject.

reperiō, -īre, repperī, repertum, (4), find.

repleō, -ēre, -ēvī, -ētum, (2), fill.

repōnō, -ere, -posuī, -positum, (3), lay, (392) ; place, (403).

requiēs, -ētis, *f.*, repose.

rēs, reī, *f.*, fortunes, (49).

reservō, (1), keep back.

resignō, (1), unseal.

resistō, -ere, -stitī, (3), stop (76).

resolvō, -ere, -solvī, -solūtum, (3), break.

resonō, (1), echo.

respiciō, -ere, -spēxī, -spĕctum, regard, (225); think of, (275).

restō, -āre, -stitī, (1), be left.

resurgō, -ere, -surrēxī, -surrēctum, (3), rise, (531).

rēte, -is, *n.*, net.

retegō, -ere, -xī, -ctum, (3), uncover, reveal.

retinācula, -ōrum, *n.*, *pl.*, mooring ropes.

retrō, *adv.*, back.

revellō, -ere, -vellī, -vulsum, (3), tear up, tear, tear away.

revinciō, -īre, -nxī, -nctum, (4), wreathe, (459).

revīsō, -ere, (3), revisit.

revocō, (1), recall.

revolvō, -ere, -volvī, -volūtum, (3) roll back; *in pass.*, fall back, (691).

rēx, rēgis, *m.*, king.

rideō, -ēre, -sī, -sum, (2), laugh, smile.

rigeō, -ēre, (2), be stiff.

rīte, *adv.*, duly, properly.

rōbur, -oris, *n.*, timber.

rogus, -ī, *m.*, pyre.

Rōmānus, -a, -um, Roman.

roscidus, -a, -um, dewy.

rūmor, -ōris, *m.*, tidings.

rumpō, -ere, -rūpī, ruptum, (3), break, burst.

ruō, -ere, ruī, rutum, (3), rush, stream, pour; rush on, (132); fall.

rursus, *adv.*, again.

rūs, rūris, *n.*, country.

sacer, -cra, -crum, sacred; dedicated, (703).

sacerdōs, -ōtis, *c.*, priest *or* priestess; priestess, (483).

sacrō, (1), dedicate.

sacrum, -ī, *n.*, sacrifice, (638); rite (50).

saepe, *adv.*, often.

saeviō, (4), rage.

saevus, -a, -um, fierce.

sagitta, -ae, *f.*, arrow.

saltem, *adv.*, at least.

saltus, -ūs, *m.*, glade, forest.

sānctus, -a, -um, holy.

sanguineus, -a, -um, bloodshot.

sanguis, -inis, *m.*, blood; stock.

sānus, -a, -um, well, healthy.

Sāturnia, -ae, *f.*, daughter of Saturn, i.e., Juno.

Sāturnius, -a, -um, Saturnian; Saturn's son, (372).

satus, -a, -um, (*from* serō), sprung.

saucius, -a, -um, wounded; Saturn's son, (372).

saxum, -ī, *n.*, rock; crag, (152).

scaena, -ae, *f.*, stage.

scēptrum, -ī, *n.*, sceptre.

scīlicet, *adv.*, forsooth, to be sure.

scōpulus, -ī, *m.*, rock.

sē *or* sēsē, himself, herself, itself; themselves.

secō, -āre, -cuī, -ctum, (1), cleave, cut.

sēcrētus, -a, -um, secret.

sēcum = cum sē.

secundus, -a, -um, favouring, favourable.

secus, *adv.*, otherwise.

sed, but.

sedeō, -ēre, sēdī, sessum (2) sit.

sēdēs, -is, *f.*, home, (10); place, (504).

sēdūcō, -ere, -xī, -ctum, (3) separate, sunder.

sēgnis, -e, slow.

sēmianimis, -e, dying.

sēmita, -ae, f., path.

sēmivir, -ī, m., effeminate.

semper, adv., always.

senex, -nis, m., old man.

sēnsus, -ūs, m., sense, feeling.

sententia, -ae, f., decision, (287).

sentiō, -īre, sēnsī, sēnsum, (4), perceive.

sepeliō, -īre, -īvī, sepultum, (4), bury.

sepulchrum, -ī, n., tomb.

sequor, -ī, secūtus sum, (3 dep.), follow ; favour, (109) ; seek, (361, 381).

serēnō, (1), calm, smooth.

Serestus, -ī, m., Serestus.

Sergestus, -ī, m., Sergestus.

sermō, -ōnis, m., speech ; gossip, (189).

serō, -ere, sēvī, satum, (3), sow, beget.

serpēns, -ntis, m., serpent.

sertum, -ī, n., garland.

serviō, (4), be a slave.

servō, (1), keep ; watch over, (485).

sēsē = sē.

seu = sīve.

sī, if ; whether, (110).

sīc, adv., thus.

siccō, (1), dry.

Sīdonius, -a, -um, Sidonian, Phoenician.

sīdus, -eris, n., star.

signum, -ī, n., sign, signal.

silēns, -ntis, silent.

sileō, (2), be silent.

silva, -ae, f., wood.

similis, -e, like.

simul, at the same time ; auke, (581).

simul ac, as soon as.

simulō, (1), pretend ; partic., simulātus, -a, -um, feigned.

sine, prep. with abl., without.

sinō, -ere, sīvī, situm, (3), allow.

sinus, -ūs, m., bosom.

sistō, ere, stitī, statum, (3),ˊstop, stay, (489) ; bring, (634).

sitis, -is, f., thirst.

sīve or seu, whether . . . or.

sociō, (1), ally.

socius, -ī, m., companion, comrade.

sol, sōlis, m., sun.

sollicitō, (1), trouble.

sōlor, (1 dep.), console.

solum, -ī, n., ground.

sōlum, adv., only.

sōlus, -a, -um, alone.

solvō, -ere, solvī, solūtum, (3), loosen ; dissolve, (55) ; free, (479) ; release, (703) ; spread, (574).

somnus, -ī, m., sleep.

sonipēs, -pedis, m., palfrey, steed.

sonō, (1), sound ; rattle, (149).

sopor, -ōris, m., sleep.

sopōrifer, -era, -erum, sleep-inducing.

soror, -ōris, f., sister.

sors, -rtis, f., oracle.

spargō, -ere, -rsī, -rsum, (3), sprinkle ; scatter, (486) ; strew, (601).

sparsus, -a, -um, partic. of foregoing, bespattered, (665).

spatior, (1 dep.), pace.

spatium, -ī, n., respite.

speciēs, -ēī, f., appearance.

specula, -ae, f., watch-tower.

spēlunca, -ae, *f.*, cave.

spernō, -ere, sprēvī, sprētum, (3), despise.

spērō, (1), hope.

spēs, -eī, *f.*, hope.

spīritus, -ūs, *m.*, breath.

spīrō, (1), breathe ; blow (562).

spolium, -ī, *n.*, spoil.

sponte, *with* meā, tuā, suā, *etc.*, of one's own accord.

spūma, -ae, *f.*, spray.

spūmō, (1), foam.

stabilis, -e, lasting.

statuō, -ere, -uī, -ūtum, (3), found, (655).

stella, -ae, *f.*, star.

stellātus, -a, -um, starred.

stimulō, (1), excite.

stīpes, -itis, *m.*, trunk (*of tree*).

stīpō, (1), throng round ; surround, (544).

stirps, -is, *f.*, progeny.

stō, -āre, stetī, statum, (1), stand.

strictus, -a, -um, drawn, (*from* stringō).

strāta, -ōrum, *n. pl.*, bed.

strīdō *or* strīdeō, -ere *or* ēre, dī, (3 *or* 2), shriek ; grate, (689).

strīdor, -ōris, *m.*, howling.

stringō, -ere, -nxī, -ctum, (3), draw.

struō, -ere, -ūxī, -ūctum, (3), build ; plan, (235, 271).

studium, -ī, *n.*, eagerness.

Stygius, -a, -um, Stygian ; Iuppiter Stygius, (638) = Pluto.

suadeō, -ere, -sī, -sum, (2), advise.

sub, *prep. with acc. and abl.*, under, beneath.

subeō, -īre, -īvī, *or* iī, -itum, uplift, (599).

subitus, -a, -um, sudden.

sublīmis, -e, high.

submittō, -ere, -mīsī, -missum, (3), subject, (414).

subnectō, -ere, -nexuī, -nexum, (3), fasten, (139).

subnītor, -ī, -nixus sum, (3 *dep.*), support.

subolēs, -is, *f.*, offspring, child.

subrīdeō, -ēre, -rīsī, -rīsum, (2), smile.

subrigō, -ere, surrēxī, surrēctum, (3), uplift.

subter, *adv.*, beneath.

succēdō, -ere, -cessī, -cessum, (3), come, (10).

succumbō, -ere, -cubuī, -cubītum, (3) bend beneath, yield.

sum, esse, fuī, be.

summa, -ae, *f.*, sum.

summittō, -ere, -mīsī, -missum, (3), subject, (414).

summus, -a, -um, topmost ; very high, (186).

sūmō, -ere, -mpsī, -mptum, (3), take.

super, *prep. with abl.*, above ; for, (233, 273) ; *adv.*, above.

superbus, -a, -um, proud.

superimpōnō, -ere, -posuī, -positum, (3), lay on top.

superus, -a, -um, upper ; *pl.*, superī, -ōrum, gods.

supīnus, -a, -um, upturned.

supplex, -icis, suppliant, humble.

supplicium, -ī, *n.*, punishment.

suprā, *prep. with acc.*, above, over

surgō, -ere, surrēxī, surrēctum, (3), rise, arise ; *partic.*, surgēns, young, (274).

suscipiŏ, -ere, -cĕpī, -ceptum, take up, raise ; bear (*children*), (327).

suspectus, -a, -um, suspect.

suspēnsus, -a, -um, anxious.

suus, -a, -um, his *or* her own, *etc.*

Sychaeus, -ī, *m.*, Sychaeus ; *as adj.*, of Sychaeus, (552).

Syrtis, -is, *f.*, Syrtis.

taceŏ, (2), be silent.

tacitus, -a, -um, silent.

taeda, -ae, *f.*, marriage-torch, torch ; pinewood, (505).

taedet, -ēre, -uit *or* taesum est, (2 *impers.*), it wearies.

tālāria, -ium, *n. pl.*, (*winged*) sandals.

tālis, -e, such.

tam, *adv.*, so ; as much.

tamen, *adv.*, nevertheless, yet.

tandem, *adv.*, at last ; pray, (349).

tangŏ, -ere, tetigī, tāctum, (3), touch ; reach, (259, 412).

tantus, -a, -um, so great, so much ; such great.

Tartara, -ōrum, *n. pl.*, Tartarus, (*a name of Hades*).

tēctum, -ī, *n.*, shelter, roof ; building, (260, 668) ; palace, (343) ; dwelling, (403).

tēcum = cum tē, with thee.

tegŏ, -ere, -xī, -ctum, (3), cover ; hide, conceal ; veil, (637).

tēla, -ae, *f.*, web.

tellūs, -ūris, *f.*, earth ; (*personified*), Earth, (166) ; land, (275).

tēlum, -ī, *n.*, missile, weapon ; shaft, (71) ; arrow, (149).

templum, -ī, *n.*, temple.

temptŏ, (1), try, probe ; assail, (413).

tempus, -oris, *n.*, time ; temple, (637).

tenāx, -ācis, tenacious.

tendŏ, -ere, tetendī, tentum *or* tēnsum, (3), stretch.

teneŏ, -ēre, -nuī, -ntum, (2), hold ; possess, (90) ; keep, (331).

tenuis, -e, thin.

ter, *adv.*, thrice.

tergeminus, -a, -um, triple.

terminus, -ī, *m.*, end.

terŏ, -ere, trīvī, trītum, (3), waste, (271).

terra, -ae, *f.*, earth, land ; (*personified*), Earth, (178).

terreŏ, (2), affright, frighten.

terribilis, -e, fearful.

terrificŏ, (1), terrify.

territŏ, (1), terrify.

testor, (1 *dep.*), call to witness.

tetigī, *see* tangŏ.

Teucer, -crī, *m.*, Teucer.

Teucrī, -ōrum, *or* -um, *m. pl.*, Trojans.

thalamus, -ī, *m.*, bridal chamber. chamber ; bridal bed, (18).

Thēbae, -ārum, *f. pl.*, Thebes.

Thȳias, (2 *syllables*), Bacchante.

tigris, -is *or* -idis, *f.*, tigress.

timeŏ, (2), fear.

timor, -ōris, *m.*, fear.

Tītān, -ānis, *m.*, Titan.

Tīthōnus, -ī, *m.*, Tithonus.

tonitrus, -ūs, *m.*, thunder.

tonŏ, (1), thunder.

torqueŏ, -ere, -rsī, -rtum, (2), twist ; toss, (583) ; hurl, (208) ; turn, (220) ; revolve, (482) ; direct, (269).

tortus, -a, -um, *partic. of* terqueō, twisted.

torus, -ī, *m.*, couch, bed.

tot, so many.

totidem, just as many.

totiēns, *adv.*, so often.

tōtus, -a, -um, whole.

trabs, -bis, *f.*, beam ; ship, (566).

tractābilis, -e, kind, (53), amenable, (439).

trādō, -ere, -didī, -ditum, (3), put, (619).

trahō, -ere, -āxī, -āctum, (3), draw ; trail, (701).

trānō, (1) swim across ; float across, (245).

trānsmittō, -ere, -mīsī, -missum, (3), cross.

trānstrum, -ī, *n.*, thwart.

tremō, -ere, -uī, (3), tremble.

trepidō, (1), tremble, quake ; hasten, (121).

trepidus, -a, -um, trembling.

trēs, tria, three.

trietēricus, -a, -um, triennial.

trīstis, -e, sad ; grim, (243).

triumphus, -ī, *m.*, triumph.

trivium, -ī, cross roads, (*junction of three roads*).

Trōia, -ae, *f.*, Troy.

Trōiānus, -a, -um, Trojan.

Trōs, -ōis, *m.*, a Trojan.

trūdō, -ere, -sī, -sum, (3), push.

tū, tuī, thou, you.

tuba, -ae, *f.*, trumpet.

tueor, (2 *dep.*), watch, watch over, gaze on.

tum, *adv.*, then.

tundō, -ere, tutudī, tūnsum, (3), buffet.

turbidus, -a, -um, troubled.

turbō, (1), stir up.

tūricremus, -a, -um, incense-burning.

turpis, -e, shameful.

turris, -is, *f.*, tower.

tūtus, -a, -um, safe, secure.

tuus, -a, -um, thy, your.

tyrannus, -ī, *m.*, lord.

Tyrius, -a, -um, Tyrian ; *as noun, m.*, a Tyrian.

Tyrus *or* Tyros, -ī, *f.*, Tyre.

ūber, -is, *n.*, udder.

ubi, *adv.*, when.

ulcīscor, -ī, ultus sum, (3 *dep.*), avenge.

ūllus, -a, -um, any.

ultimus, -a, -um, last, remotest.

ultor, -ōris, *m.*, avenger.

ultrīx, -īcis, *f.*, avenging.

ultrō, *adv.*, first, (304).

ululātus, -ūs, *m.*, wailing.

ululō, (1), cry approval, (168) ; howl.

umbra, -ae, *f.*, shade, shadow ; darkness, (7) ; apparition, (571) ; ghost, (386).

ūmēns, (*partic. of* ūmeō), wet dewy.

umerus, -ī, *m.*, shoulder.

ūmidus, -a, -um, moist, (486).

umquam, *adv.*, ever.

ūnā, *adv.*, together.

ūnanimus, -a, -um, of one mind with.

unda, -ae, *f.*, wave.

undique, *adv.*, from all sides.

undōsus, -a, -um, billowy.

unguis, -is, *m.*, nail.

unguō, -ere, -nxī, -nctum, (3), anoint, oil ; ūnctus, (398), *perhaps* greased, *to facilitate launching.*